Third Edition

Workbook to Accompany Understanding Medical Coding

A Comprehensive Guide

Sandra L. Johnson, MS, CPC, CMA (AAMA)

Robin I. Linker, CHCA, CHCAS, CPC-1, CCS-P, CPC-H, MCS-P, CPC-P, CHC

DELMAR
CENGAGE Learning

Australia • Brazil • Japan • Mexico • Singapore • Span • United Kingdom • United States

Workbook to Accompany
Understanding Medical Coding:
A Comprehensive Guide, third edition
Sandra L. Johnson
Robin I. Linker

Vice President, Careers & Computing: Dave Garza

Director of Learning Solutions: Matthew Kane

Executive Editor: Rhonda Dearborn

Managing Editor: Marah Bellegarde

Associate Product Manager: Meghan E. Orvis

Editorial Assistant: Lauren Whalen

Vice President, Marketing: Jennifer Ann Baker

Marketing Director: Wendy E. Mapstone

Senior Marketing Manager: Nancy Bradshaw

Senior Director, Education Production:
Wendy A. Troeger

Production Manager: Andrew Crouth

Senior Content Project Manager:
Kara A. DiCaterino

Senior Art Director: Jack Pendleton

For product information and technology assistance, contact us at
Cengage Learning Customer & Sales Support, 1-800-354-9706

For permission to use material from this text or product,
submit all requests online at **www.cengage.com/permissions**.
Further permissions questions can be e-mailed to
permissionrequest@cengage.com

Library of Congress Control Number: 2011935706

ISBN-13: 978-1-111-30681-6

ISBN-10: 1-111-30681-8

Delmar
5 Maxwell Drive
Clifton Park, NY 12065-2919
USA

Cengage Learning is a leading provider of customized learning solutions with office locations around the globe, including Singapore, the United Kingdom, Australia, Mexico, Brazil, and Japan. Locate your local office at: **international.cengage.com/region**

Cengage Learning products are represented in Canada by Nelson Education, Ltd.

To learn more about Delmar, visit **www.cengage.com/delmar**

Purchase any of our products at your local college store or at our preferred online store **www.cengagebrain.com**

Notice to the Reader
Publisher does not warrant or guarantee any of the products described herein or perform any independent analysis in connection with any of the product information contained herein. Publisher does not assume, and expressly disclaims, any obligation to obtain and include information other than that provided to it by the manufacturer. The reader is expressly warned to consider and adopt all safety precautions that might be indicated by the activities described herein and to avoid all potential hazards. By following the instructions contained herein, the reader willingly assumes all risks in connection with such instructions. The publisher makes no representations or warranties of any kind, including but not limited to, the warranties of fitness for particular purpose or merchantability, nor are any such representations implied with respect to the material set forth herein, and the publisher takes no responsibility with respect to such material. The publisher shall not be liable for any special, consequential, or exemplary damages resulting, in whole or part, from the readers' use of, or reliance upon, this material.

Printed in the United States of America
1 2 3 4 5 6 7 16 15 14 13 12

Table of Contents

Introduction to Coding

1

The *Occupational Outlook Handbook,* published by the U.S. Department of Labor–Bureau of Labor Statistics, predicts an increasing demand for careers in the field of health information management, including coders, insurance specialists, and billing and reimbursement specialists. Employment opportunities for these careers exist in medical practices, hospitals, insurance companies, government agencies, and private coding and billing services. Those with experience in these areas can also work as consultants, educators, auditors, and trainers.

Training requirements include knowledge of anatomy and physiology, medical terminology, coding (including ICD-9-CM, CPT, and HCPCS), critical thinking, and computer and data entry skills. Once the initial training is accomplished, certification and membership in one or more professional associations, as well as maintaining a professional credential, are not only recommended but often required. Some of these associations are the American Association of Professional Coders (AAPC), American Health Information Management Association (AHIMA), and the Board of Medical Specialty Coding and Compliance (BMSC). The National Electronic Billers Alliance (NEBA) and the American Medical Billing Association (AMBA) are associations providing credentials to claim and reimbursement specialists. The Association of Health Care Auditors and Educators (AHCAE) offers credentialing in chart auditing as well as the AAPC.

Individuals working in all areas of health care, including coding and billing, must recognize instances of fraudulent and abusive activity and be aware of the organizations to be notified of these activities: HIPAA, OIG, OBRA, and CMS.

As we approach the transition of ICD-9-CM to ICD-10-CM on October 1, 2013, plans for this transition must be in place This workbook includes new practice exercises for ICD-10-CM.

Name: _____   **Date:** _____

FRAUD AND ABUSE

Chapter 1 defines fraud and abuse using the definitions provided by the Health Insurance Portability and Account-ability Act (HIPAA) of 1996, as well as OIG, OBRA, and CMS.

Fraud and Abuse Review Questions

Identify the following activities as "abuse" (A) or "fraud" (F).

_____ 1. A simple wound repair of a laceration to the forehead is coded complex in order to receive higher reimbursement.

_____ 2. The date for symptoms related to a preexisting condition is changed so the patient may qualify for insurance benefits.

_____ 3. A primary care physician refers all female patients to a gynecologist for routine pelvic/breast exam and Pap smear.

_____ 4. The laboratory components of a comprehensive metabolic panel are coded and billed individually instead of using the panel code.

_____ 5. A physician refers patients to a particular pharmacy in order to receive a discount on medications ordered and used in the office.

_____ 6. An internationally known manufacturer recognized for its cardiac products offers a cardiovascular surgeon and the clinic staff an all-expense-paid trip to Aruba for the exclusive use of its products.

_____ 7. Refunds are not issued for services determined to be not reasonable and necessary by Medicare.

_____ 8. An uninsured patient seen in the Emergency Department "borrows" a friend's insurance card to receive medical care.

_____ 9. A medical office bills for telephone calls for prescription refills without advance notification to the patient.

_____ 10. A medical practice finds it is easier to routinely bill the patient for copayment instead of collecting it at the time of service.

MEDICAL TERMINOLOGY

An essential aspect of medical coding is the use of medical terminology. ICD-9-CM, CPT, and HCPCS code books utilize medical terms; therefore, a medical coder must be knowledgeable in the language of medicine and its usage, as well as the anatomy of the human body.

Medical Terminology Review Questions

Select the correct term for the following.

1. What is the medical term for an obstetrical or vaginal repair?

   a. Colpectomy   c. Vaginectomy

   b. Episiotomy   d. Vaginorrhaphy

2. What is cholecystitis with cholelithiasis?

   a. Inflammation of the gallbladder with gallstones

   b. Inflammation of the stomach and lower intestinal tract

   c. Ulceration of the colon

   d. Internal and external hemorrhoids

3. What is the medical term for removal of the eye?

   a. Enucleation

   b. Evacuation

   c. Ophthalmoscopy

   d. Orbitectomy

4. What is the medical term for removal of fluid from the knee joint?

   a. Arthrocentesis

   b. Arthrodesis

   c. Arthoplasty

   d. Arthroscopy

5. What is an ileus?

   a. Inflammation of the hip bone

   b. Intestinal inflammation

   c. Intestinal obstruction

   d. Skin disorder

6. What does gastrodynia mean?

   a. Abdominal fissure

   b. Abdominal pain

   c. Intestinal virus

   d. Rectal spasm

7. In the diagnosis "carcinoma of the liver metastatic to the pancreas," what does metastatic mean?

   a. The cancer has spread to the liver.

   b. The cancer has spread to the pancreas.

   c. The cancer is in remission.

   d. The cancer is in terminal stages.

8. What is the meaning of glossopharyngeal?

   a. Pertaining to the mouth and throat

   b. Pertaining to the tongue and throat

   c. Pertaining to the esophagus and throat

   d. Pertaining to the glands and throat

9. The term keratin refers to what anatomical system?

   a. Endocrinology

   b. Female reproductive

   c. Integumentary

   d. Musculoskeletal

10. What does the term gravida mean?

   a. A benign lesion

   b. A pregnant woman

   c. The weight of a substance

   d. Transplanting skin or tissue

11. What term means a specimen is visible to the naked eye?

   a. Gross

   b. Insulate

   c. Isolate

   d. Microscopic

12. What is onychocryptosis?

   a. Excessive granulation tissue

   b. Inflamed hair follicle

   c. Infection of an ingrown nail

   d. Skin rash

13. What is hematemesis?

    a. Blood in urine

    b. Coughing up blood

    c. Rectal bleeding

    d. Vomiting of blood

14. What is melena?

    a. Blood in sputum

    b. Blood in stools

    c. Blood in urine

    d. Blood in nasal drainage

15. What is the medical term for painful menstruation?

    a. Amenorrhea

    b. Dysplasia

    c. Dysmenorrhea

    d. Menometrorrhagia

EXERCISES

Review Questions

Visit the AAPC website at http://www.aapc.com and answer the following questions.

1. List the areas of certification offered by the American Academy of Professional Coders (AAPC).

    a.

    b.

    c.

2. List examples of how to obtain preapproved CEUs offered by the AAPC.

    a.

    b.

    c.

    d.

    e.

3. AAPC offers specialty credentials. Visit the AAPC website at http://aapc.com to identify these credentials and compare areas covered in each specialty exam.

    _____

    _____

4. Visit the American Hospital Information Management Association (AHIMA) website at http://www.ahima.org. Compare the coding CCS and CCS-P credentials of AHIMA with the CPC and CPC-H of AAPC.

    _____

    _____

5. Advanced coding certification is available through the Board of Medical Specialty Coding (BSMC). Visit their website at http://www.medicalspecialtycoding.com for information on advanced coding specialist (ACS) credentials available in a variety of specialties. What is the purpose or advantage of seeking an ACS credential?

_____

_____

MEDICAL NECESSITY

Documentation in a medical record must be complete, legible, and accurate to appropriately assign evaluation and management codes and link them to the correct ICD-9-CM codes to support medical necessity for the service or procedure provided.

Medical Necessity Review Questions

In the following list of terms, link the correct diagnosis to the appropriate service or procedures needed to support medical necessity to the insurance company.

Diagnosis

_____ 1. Chest pain

_____ 2. Neoplasm of breast

_____ 3. Type II diabetes

_____ 4. Pneumonia

_____ 5. Anemia

_____ 6. Severe prolapse of eyelids

_____ 7. Fracture

_____ 8. Dysuria and pyuria

_____ 9. Hypercholesterolemia

_____ 10. Superficial skin abrasion

_____ 11. Coronary artery disease

_____ 12. Family history of colon cancer

_____ 13. Chronic otitis media

_____ 14. Hematuria

_____ 15. Sore throat

_____ 16. Impacted cerumen

_____ 17. Coagulation disorder/on blood thinner

Procedure/Service

A. EEG

B. Ear lavage

C. Myringotomy

D. EKG

E. Colonoscopy

F. Fasting glucose

G. Strep test

H. Mastectomy

I. Chest X-ray

J. Blepharoplasty

K. TURP

L. Pulmonary function study

M. Nasal packing

N. CBC

O. Debridement

P. Prothrombin time

Q. Closed reduction of femur

Diagnosis

_____ 18. Positive PPD/TB skin test

_____ 19. Epistaxis

_____ 20. Prostatic hypertrophy/urinary retention

_____ 21. Seizure disorder

_____ 22. COPD

_____ 23. Burn of forearm, partial treatment with dressing

_____ 24. Carcinoma of colon

_____ 25. Pleurisy

Procedure/Service

R. Urinalysis

S. Lipid panel

T. Cardiac catheterization

ICD-9-CM

2

ICD-9-CM contains codes for diagnoses, symptoms, illnesses, and diseases. Volume 1 contains the tabular numerical listing of diagnosis codes. Volume 2 contains the alphabetic listing of diagnoses. All health care facilities use Volumes 1 and 2 for coding the reason for the patient's encounter, whether it takes place in the physician office, hospital, nursing facility, or as part of in-home care. Volume 3 contains a tabular and alphabetic listing of procedures that are primarily used in the hospital inpatient setting. This textbook will focus on Volumes 1 and 2.

Volume 1, the Classification of Diseases and Injuries, contains 17 chapters grouped according to the cause or body system, such as neoplasms. V codes, E codes, and M codes are also included in Volume 1.

Since Volume 2 contains the alphabetic index, the coder must look in this volume first to locate the code for the diagnosis or reason the patient has presented for a medical encounter. The code is then verified in the numerical list of Volume 1. It is important to always cross-check the term in Volume 1 with the description of the term in Volume 2 in order to verify the code and to check the fifth-digit requirement. Chapter 2 of the textbook describes the steps to follow in locating the main term, identifying subterms, and verifying the code in the tabular list.

V codes can be used to describe the reason for the patient's visit when the patient is not sick or does not have a medical complaint. Many of these codes are used to code routine services, a family or personal history of a condition, and screening or testing when a patient is exposed to a disease or illness.

E codes represent external causes of injury and are used as secondary codes to show the reason for an injury, such as an automobile accident or a fall. E codes are also used to report poisonings, toxic effects of substances, or drug overdoses.

M codes, or morphology codes, are used primarily by cancer registries to identify a neoplasm's cell type and behavior in conjunction with the neoplasm code from the neoplasm table. M codes are not used for insurance reimbursement reporting purposes.

Name: _____   **Date:** _____

EXERCISES

Coding Exercises

Code the following exercises using Volumes 1 and 2 of ICD-9-CM.

1. Mass in breast _____

2. Shadow on lung seen on chest X-ray, etiology undetermined _____

3. History of allergy to penicillin _____

4. Carcinoma of sigmoid colon metastatic to peritoneum _____ _____

5. Migraine headache _____

6. Internal and external thrombosed hemorrhoids _____ _____

7. Diabetic skin ulcer in patient with Type II diabetes _____ _____

8. Carbuncle of eyelid _____

9. Chest pain, probable angina pectoris _____

10. Positive tuberculin test _____

11. Benign growth of labia majora _____

12. Diabetic gangrene _____ _____

13. Carcinoma in situ of the cervix uteri _____

14. Amenorrhea _____

15. Benign hypertrophy of prostate _____

Certification Questions

1. Which one of the following is an example of an eponym?

   a. Alzheimer's disease

   b. Epistaxis

   c. Seborrheic dermatitis

   d. Syncope

2. A malignant neoplasm is removed from the lower-outer quadrant of the right breast. There is metastasis to the right lung. What are the correct codes?

   a. 174.5, 162.9

   b. 174.5, 197.0

   c. 174.9, 197.0

   d. 239.3, 239.1

3. A laboratory report indicated an abnormal result on a patient's Mantoux test required for his employment in a nursing facility. What is the correct code?

   a. 010.90

   b. 795.5

   c. 795.79

   d. V74.1

4. A 49-year-old patient is in the office complaining of severe chest pain. An acute MI is suspected, but a conclusive diagnosis is pending additional studies to be done at the hospital. Until a definite diagnosis has been determined, how would this situation be coded in the office for the physician's bill?

    a. 410.90   c. 786.50

    b. 786.5   d. 786.59

5. A patient is brought into the Emergency Department for syncope and hypotension. After examination and testing, no medical reason can be determined for the symptoms. What are the correct codes?

    a. 780.09, 458.9   c. 780.2, 458.9

    b. 780.2, 401.9   d. 780.4, 458.9

6. An AIDS patient is seen in the office with skin lesions over his back indicative of Kaposi's sarcoma. An incisional biopsy confirms this diagnosis. What are the correct codes?

    a. 042, 176.0   c. 042, 709.9

    b. 042, 176.9   d. 042, 709.9, 176.0

7. A patient is in the office complaining of involuntary movement of her legs accompanied by an itchy feeling, especially at night when she goes to bed. The diagnosis today is restless leg syndrome. What is the correct code?

    a. 333.90   c. 781.0

    b. 333.94   d. 799.2

8. A patient with seriously out-of-control Type I diabetes mellitus is admitted for regulation of his insulin dosage. He also complains of some chest discomfort. The patient had been in the hospital four weeks earlier for an acute myocardial infarction of the inferoposterior wall, and an EKG is performed to check the patient's current cardiac status. What are the correct codes for the most recent visit?

    a. 250.00, 410.32   c. 250.03, 410.30

    b. 250.03, 410.32   d. 250.80, 410.32

9. A patient is scheduled for outpatient testing for complaints of urinary retention and enlargement of the prostate. He returns to the office for follow-up and to receive the results after the tests are completed. The diagnosis is adenocarcinoma of the prostate with metastasis to the bone. What are the correct codes?

    a. 185, 198.5   c. 239.5, 170.9

    b. 185, 198.5, M8010/6   d. 239.5, 170.9, M8010/6

10. A housekeeper cleaning a room in the hospital is exposed to blood-tainted emesis. What is the correct code?

    a. 578.0   c. V01.9

    b. 994.9   d. V15.85

Review Questions

1. Explain the steps used to code a patient's complaint of diarrhea.

    _____

    _____

2. Explain the difference between a principal diagnosis and a first-listed diagnosis.

   _____

   _____

3. NOS is an abbreviation used in ICD-9-CM to indicate unspecified when the _____ has no further information to fully define or describe the condition.

4. NEC is an abbreviation used in ICD-9-CM to indicate a more specific category is not available in

   _____.

5. Indicate which of the following is identified as a V code by placing an "x" in the space provided.

   _____ a. Nausea, vomiting, abdominal pain

   _____ b. Exposure to patient with tuberculosis

   _____ c. Annual gynecological exam with Pap smear

   _____ d. Elevated blood pressure reading

   _____ e. Flu vaccination

   _____ f. Abnormal electrocardiogram

   _____ g. Encounter for contraceptive counseling and management

   _____ h. Family history of breast carcinoma

   _____ i. Normal pregnancy

   _____ j. Screening for hyperthyroidism

ICD-10-CM Coding

Assign ICD-10-CM codes for the following scenarios.

1. A 22-year-old patient presents with symptoms of jaundice and swelling of the liver. Exam and lab studies determine the patient to have hepatitis A.

   _____

2. A patient recently returned from a planned vacation. However, while there he found himself in the middle of a military war zone. The patient is now experiencing difficulty sleeping, anxiety, and depression, which are determined to be related to this acute crisis.

   _____

3. A six-year-old child is seen by the pediatrician for behavioral problems, such as the inability to sit still, pay attention, and follow directions. The child's teacher has recommended medical intervention as she suspects attention-deficit/hyperactivity disorder. After thorough examination and evaluation, the child is diagnosed with attention deficit hyperactive disorder.

    _____

4. A 41-year-old female is diagnosed with carcinoma in situ of the right breast. There is a family history of lung cancer.

    _____

5. A patient is seen in the office with the complaint of severe headaches occurring on a daily basis. An EEG and MRI are performed and have ruled out the possibility of a brain tumor.

    _____

HCPCS Level II

3

The Healthcare Common Procedure Coding System (HCPCS) is a three-level coding system. HCPCS Level I is AMA/CPT. HCPCS Level II, maintained by the Centers for Medicare and Medicaid Services (CMS), contains national codes used to identify procedures, supplies, medications (with the exception of vaccines), equipment, and miscellaneous items. Vaccines and immunizations are assigned CPT codes.

There are multiple sections of HCPCSII such as the following:

Transportation Services	A0000–A0999
Medical and Surgical Supplies	A4000–A8999
Miscellaneous and Experimental	A9000–A9999
Enteral and Parenteral Therapy	B4000–B9999
Hospital Outpatient PPS	C1030–C9899
Dental Procedures *(This information varies by publisher as to inclusion.)*	D0000–D9999
Durable Medical Equipment (DME)	E0100–E9999
Professional Health Care Procedures and Services *(codes that would otherwise be coded in CPT but for which there are not CPT codes)*	G0000–G9999
Rehabilitative Services	H0001–H2037
Drugs Administered other than Oral Method	J0000–J8999
Chemotherapy Drugs	J9000–J9999
Temporary Codes for DMERCS (Durable Medical Equipment Regional Carriers)	K0000–K9999
Orthotic Procedures	L0100–L4999
Prosthetic Procedures	L5000–L9999
Medical Services	M0000–M0301
Pathology and Laboratory	P0000–P9999
Temporary Codes	Q0035–Q9968
Diagnostic Radiology Services	R0000–R5999

Temporary National Codes	S0000–S9999
State Medicaid Agency Codes	T1000–T9999
Vision Services	V0000–V2799
Hearing Services	V5008–V5299

When assigning codes for drugs, both generic and trade names are listed, although codes are assigned to the generic names. The brand or trade names are referred to the proper generic name. Close attention must be paid to the amount column that refers to the amount of drug dispensed in order to assign the correct code. It is also important to know the various routes of administration of a drug:

IA	Intra-arterial	INH	Inhalation
IV	Intravenous	INJ	Injection not otherwise specified
IM	Intramuscular	VAR	Various routes
IT	Intrathecal	OTH	Other routes
SC	Subcutaneous	ORAL	Administered orally

Name: _____   **Date:** _____

EXERCISES

Coding Exercises

Assign HCPCSII codes to the following.

1. Inhalation of nasal vaccine   _____

2. Morphine 10 mg IV   _____

3. Hearing aid assessment   _____

4. Adjustable aluminum quad prong cane   _____

5. Alcohol wipes, per box   _____

6. Emergency ambulance service, advanced life support (ALS1-emergency)   _____

7. Vitamin B12 800 mcg IM   _____

8. Silicone breast prosthesis, no integral adhesive   _____

9. Mobile commode chair with detachable arms   _____

10. Cast supplies, long arm splint, adult (11+ years), plaster   _____

11. Sign language interpreter, 30 minutes   _____

12. Mitomycin 25 mg for IV chemotherapy   _____

13. Two units red blood cells for transfusion   _____

14. Portable EKG transported to nursing facility, one patient   _____

15. Routine transportation of patient in wheelchair van   _____

Certification Questions

1. The physician orders Valium 5 mg to be administered to a patient IM. HCPCSII lists the code by generic name. What is the generic name for Valium?

   a. Diazepam   c. Haloperidol

   b. Furosemide   d. Lorazepam

2. An 18-year-old female comes into the OB/GYN clinic for an injection of Depo-Provera 150 mg for contraceptive purposes. What is the correct code?

   a. J1000   c. J1055

   b. J1051 x 3   d. J1056

3. A 55-year-old female, diagnosed with breast cancer, undergoes a unilateral simple mastectomy with implantation of a silicone prosthesis. What is the correct code?

   a. L8020   c. L8600

   b. L8030   d. L8699

4. A patient is given injectable Bicillin L-A 200,000 units IM for strep throat. What is the correct code?

    a. J0558   c. J0594 x 100

    b. J0561   d. J0561 x 2

5. A patient is critically injured in a motorcycle accident. When emergency medical technicians arrive, preparation is made to stat-flight the patient by helicopter to a trauma center in a nearby city. What is the correct code?

    a. A0422   c. A0430

    b. A0427   d. A0431

6. A patient has a strange lesion removed in the physician office. A surgical tray is used for this procedure and the provider wants to bill for it. The specimen is sent to pathology for testing. What is the best code to use when reporting the surgical tray?

    a. 11200   c. 99070

    b. 88304   d. A4550

7. Which one of the following is an example of an inhalation drug?

    a. Albuterol   c. Estradiol valerate

    b. Amitriptyline   d. Phenobarbital

8. What category of HCPCSII codes is developed and recognized by commercial payers, such as Blue Cross Blue Shield?

    a. A codes   c. S codes

    b. C codes   d. T codes

9. A hospital bed with electric head, foot, and height adjustments, including mattress and side rails, is rented for home use. What is the correct code?

    a. E0250-RR   c. E0260-RR

    b. E0255-RR   d. E0265-RR

10. A 52-year-old male with Type II diabetes is fitted for a custom-prepared and molded shoe from a cast of the patient's foot. What is the correct code?

    a. A5500   c. A5507

    b. A5501   d. A5510

Review Questions

1. Match the route of medication administration with the correct term.

    _____ Intrathecal   A. Within the muscle

    _____ Intravenous   B. p.o. (by mouth)

    _____ Subcutaneous   C. Within a sheath

    _____ Inhalation   D. Within a vein

    _____ Intramuscular   E. Beneath the layers of the skin

    _____ Oral   F. Breathing in

2. In what section of HCPCSII would you locate the code for a CPAP device?

   a. Durable medical equipment
   c. Orthotic procedures

   b. Medical and surgical supplies
   d. Rehabilitative services

3. Which one of the following is a DME?

   a. Blood glucose monitor
   c. Ostomy supplies

   b. Dentures
   d. Vascular catheters

4. What CPT code is used for all supplies, medications, and equipment not applicable to HCPCSII? What must be attached with the claim to obtain reimbursement?

   _____

   _____

5. Which one of the following is an example of a diagnostic radiology service?

   a. Enteral nutrition infusion pump
   c. Screening Pap smear

   b. Portable X-ray equipment with personnel to nursing facility
   d. Venipuncture for collection of specimen

ICD-10-CM Coding

Assign ICD-10-CM codes for the following scenarios.

1. The patient returns to have his pulse generator rechecked again as it continues to malfunction. The technician and physician both determine the problem to be a battery breakdown and schedule a time for replacement. How should this mechanical malfunction be coded?

   _____

   _____

2. Following a failed hearing screening, the patient returns for a formal hearing evaluation. How should the return visit be coded?

   _____

   _____

3. A 72-year-old was rushed to the ER with strange, sharp abdominal pains. After careful examination and scans, it is determined that the pain is actually a small liver laceration that will be watched carefully. Code the final diagnosis.

   _____

   _____

4. A 49-year-old male complaining of chest pains presents to the cardiologist for a possible heart attack. The cardiologist determines the patient is suffering from spasm-induced angina caused by working in an environment where he is exposed to heavy tobacco smoke all day long. How should this be coded?

   _____

   _____

5. A newborn with a congenital birth defect to both arms was given a diagnosis of lobster-claw hands. How should this be coded?

   _____

   _____

Current Procedural Terminology (CPT) Basics

4

Current Procedural Terminology (CPT) is a five-digit numerical code used to describe specific medical services and procedures performed by physicians and other health care providers. First introduced in 1966, the current edition is referred to as CPT-4.

Knowledge of medical terminology is necessary to assign codes to services and procedures to a third-party payer and to link ICD-9-CM codes to prove medical necessity.

CPT is divided into six sections: Evaluation and Management, Anesthesia, Surgery, Radiology, Pathology and Laboratory, and Medicine. A listing of Category II and III codes, Appendices A–N, and the Index are included. Modifiers are two-digit numbers added to the basic CPT code to indicate special circumstances in the description of the CPT code.

Name: _____   **Date:** _____

EXERCISES

Coding Exercises

Assign codes to the following using the index and all chapters of CPT. Assign a modifier as indicated.

1. Puncture aspiration of cyst of breast   _____
2. I&D of an infected thyroglossal duct cyst   _____
3. Complete X-ray of the scapula   _____
4. I&D hematoma of right wrist   _____
5. Patient visit for a blood pressure check only by nurse ordered
   by the physician   _____
6. Laryngoscopy endoscopy, indirect   _____
7. Neuroplasty for carpal tunnel syndrome of the median nerve   _____
8. Complete radiological exam of the mandible   _____
9. Incisional biopsy of testis   _____
10. Intradermal test for tuberculosis   _____
11. Medical testimony by a physician   _____
12. Tonsillectomy and adenoidectomy on a 15-year-old   _____
13. Office visit (expanded problem-focused Level 2) for a patient last
    seen five years ago   _____
14. Flexible colonoscopy with biopsy   _____

Certification Questions

Select the proper CPT codes.

1. A patient is seen in the office for a needle biopsy of the testis for suspected testicular carcinoma.
   a. 54500
   b. 99202, 54505
   c. 99212, 54500
   d. 99212, 10021

2. The patient later undergoes a simple bilateral orchiectomy.
   a. 54520-50
   b. 54522-50
   c. 54530-50
   d. 54520

3. A 16-year-old male is seen in the Emergency Department for a laceration of the scalp measuring 3.5 cm. A problem-focused history and exam are performed with an intermediate repair of the laceration.
   a. 99281-47, 12002
   b. 99281-25, 12013
   c. 99281-25, 12032
   d. 99282-47, 12052

4. A four-year-old patient is evaluated in the urgent care center for an injury to the left leg. An X-ray is taken of the tibia and fibula (two views), which confirms a fracture. The patient is referred to an orthopedic surgeon for treatment. Code the X-ray service.

   a. 73590-LT

   b. 73590-RT

   c. 73592-LT

   d. 73550-LT

5. A patient is referred to the hospital laboratory for an electrolyte panel, automated CBC with automated differential WBC, and a nonautomated urinalysis with microscopy. Code the labs.

   a. 80051, 85004, 81000

   b. 80051, 85025, 81000

   c. 80051, 85025, 81001

   d. 80051, 85027, 81000

6. A new patient is seen in the office for infection of the left great toe. The patient also has Type II diabetes mellitus. An expanded problem-focused office visit and a problem-focused exam is performed. During the encounter, the provider decides to perform an I&D of the great toe abscess.

   a. 99201-25, 10060

   b. 99212, 10060, 99070

   c. 99202-25, 10061, 99070

   d. 99201, 10160, 99070

7. Referring to the case in question 6, this patient returns for recheck of the infected area three days later. The area has healed well with no additional treatment today. He does have blood drawn for a glucose to be sent to the laboratory.

   a. 99202, 36415

   b. 99024, 36415

   c. 99212, 36415, 82947

   d. 99212, 82947

8. An established patient is admitted to the hospital on Monday, followed in the hospital on Tuesday, with discharge on Wednesday. Hospital admission and subsequent visit are all low levels with straightforward medical decision making. The planning and management to discharge the patient take 25 minutes. Code the hospital stay.

   a. 99218, 99217

   b. 99221, 99231, 99238

   c. 99221, 99231, 99239

   d. 99234, 99238

9. Dr. Smith assists Dr. Brown with a craniotomy for drainage of an intracranial abscess. Code for the assist.

   a. 61320

   b. 61320-80

   c. 61546-78

   d. 61570-8

10. As a new patient to the practice, a 45-year-old patient is seen for a comprehensive physical examination. He has no complaints. He will return as needed (prn).

    a. 99204

    b. 99205

    c. 99244

    d. 99386

Review Questions

1. List the six sections of CPT.

   _____ _____

   _____ _____

   _____ _____

2. What edition is the current publication of CPT? _____

3. What does the + symbol indicate in CPT?
   a. Add-on code
   b. Modifier
   c. Multiple codes
   d. New code

4. Where can a list of all modifiers be located in CPT?
   a. Appendix A
   b. Appendix B
   c. Appendix C
   d. Appendix D

5. Match the following abbreviations with their respective definitions.

   _____ECG   A. Certification credential in coding

   _____I&D   B. AMA's procedural reference for physicians

   _____E/M   C. Electrocardiogram

   _____CPT   D. Form used to file medical claims

   _____ICD-9-CM   E. Section of CPT dedicated to patient evaluations

   _____CMS   F. Surgical technique used to expel contents

   _____CMS-1500   G. Federal agency that administers Medicare/Medicaid

   _____CPC   H. Diagnostic code-set used for classification

Evaluation and Management

The first section of CPT introduces Evaluation and Management (E/M) codes. These codes are used for provider services based on the examination of the patient in various settings, such as an office, hospital, Emergency Department, or nursing facility.

Documentation in the medical record is a key factor in selecting an appropriate CPT code, as well as the correct ICD-9-CM code. Questions such as who, what, when, where, and why are essential to assigning codes. *REMEMBER: If it is not documented, it did not happen!*

Name: _____　　　　**Date:** _____

EXERCISES

Coding Exercises

Assign E/M codes to the following.

1. Detailed consultation, new patient (pt.), inpatient　　　　　　　　　_____

2. Well-child checkup, established (est.) pt., age seven　　　　　　　_____

3. Office consultation, new pt., second opinion request by mother of child for tonsillectomy/adenoidectomy　　　　　　　　　　　_____

4. Office visit, est. pt., expanded problem-focused (EPF) history and exam, LC-medical decision making　　　　　　　　　　　　_____

5. Admission to hospital, initial hospital care, straightforward, detailed history and exam　　　　　　　　　　　　　　　_____

6. Subsequent hospital care, medical decision of moderate complexity, and expanded problem-focused exam　　　　　　　　　　_____

7. Hospital discharge, 30 minutes to discuss medications　　　　　_____

8. Emergency Department care, minimal care required, PF, straightforward　_____

9. Initial inpatient consultation, new pt., moderate complexity, comprehensive history and exam　　　　　　　　　　　　　_____

10. Initial office consultation, medical decision of high complexity, comprehensive workup for transplant surgery consideration　　　　　_____

11. Rest home visit, evaluation of est. pt., moderate complexity, EPF exam　_____

12. Admission to skilled nursing facility, detailed history, comprehensive exam, moderate decision making　　　　　　　　　　　_____

13. Patient admitted to typical postop observation area following laparoscopic cholecystectomy at 10 a.m. with discharge 5 p.m. same day　　_____

14. New pt. with EPF exam and history, seen in urgent care with low-complexity decision making　　　　　　　　　　　　　_____

15. Pediatric critical care, initial, inpatient, age nine months　　　_____

Certification Questions

1. An established patient was seen by the CMA to have his blood pressure checked. BP today is 140/90, which is lower than the last BP check one week ago. He will return in one week for recheck. Select the proper code.

   a. 99211　　　　　　　　　　c. 99241

   b. 99212　　　　　　　　　　d. 99201

2. A patient was seen by her family physician with a recommendation to have a hysterectomy. The patient consulted another physician for a second opinion. How is this visit coded?

    a. Patient office visit

    b. A follow-up consultation

    c. An expanded problem-focused office visit for a new patient

    d. An initial office consultation

3. What is the correct modifier to use when a consultation is required by a third party?

    a. -22

    b. -32

    c. -54

    d. -57

4. An 87-year-old female was admitted to the nursing home after discharge from the hospital for management and physical therapy for a fracture of the left femur. Her primary care physician came by the facility to discharge the patient after four weeks to home care, spending 20 minutes with the patient and her family. How is this coded?

    a. 99217

    b. 99238

    c. 99315

    d. 99316

5. A physician in the Emergency Department (ED) of a hospital examines an 18-year-old with the complaint of recurrent, severe menstrual migraine headache. A brief history of the present illness is taken and a complete review of systems given. Examination is limited to the neurological and musculoskeletal system. Medications administered in the ED significantly relieve the patient's symptoms. How is this coded?

    a. 99241

    b. 99281

    c. 99282

    d. 99284

6. The WC insurance physician performs an independent medical examination to determine and rate impairment for disability for workers' compensation benefits. How is this coded?

    a. 99450

    b. 99455

    c. 99456

    d. 99420

7. A patient is seen for follow-up in the office for postop mastectomy with an expanded problem-focused visit and examination focused on newly detected diabetes and treatment. How is this coded?

    a. 99202-58

    b. 99214-24

    c. 99213-24

    d. 99214-58

8. A patient is admitted to the hospital's observation area to monitor elevated blood pressure readings following a minor surgical procedure. The patient is discharged home later the same day to be followed by the primary care physician. How is this coded?

    a. 99218, 99217

    b. 99221, 99238

    c. 99234

    d. 99234, 99238

9. An OB/GYN counsels a group of 12 teenagers regarding STDs and their prevention. Their session lasts 30 minutes. How is this coded?

    a. 99401

    b. 99402 x 12

    c. 99411

    d. 99403

10. A construction worker was seen in the ED for acute eye pain associated with a possible steel shaving in the affected eye. A problem-focused exam of the eye shows no sign of a foreign body. Over-the-counter eye drops are advised. How is this coded?

   a. 99281

   b. 99282

   c. 99283

   d. 99284

Review Questions

1. The CPT E/M guidelines define a new patient as one who has not received professional services from the physician or another physician of the same specialty in the same group practice within the past _____ years.

2. List the three key components of documentation required in order to assign an E/M code.

   _____

   _____

   _____

3. Which series of E/M codes is selected for consultations initiated by the patient and/or family in the office setting?

   a. 99241–99245

   b. 99218–99220

   c. 99201–99215

   d. 99251–99255

4. What criteria are required in the time element of selecting critical care codes?

   _____

   _____

   _____

5. Emergency Department visits are coded in the Emergency Department section of Evaluation and Management. What section is used to code visits to urgent/immediate care centers?

   _____

ICD-10-CM Coding

Assign ICD-10-CM codes for the following scenarios.

1. A four-year-old well-child check proved the child to be right on target and without any abnormalities. How should the provider code this service?

   _____

   _____

2. Mr. Tate continues to have difficulty driving at night as his vision is vastly different from driving in the daylight. The ophthalmologist has diagnosed him with night blindness and has recommended he refrain from driving past dark. What code should the ophthalmologist use?

   _____

   _____

3. After undergoing a mastoidectomy of the left ear, the patient is now suffering from chronic inflammation determined to be caused by the surgery. How should this be coded?

_____

_____

4. After several rheumatological tests were performed and proved normal, the physician determined the patient to have fibromyalgia. How should this be coded?

_____

_____

5. The patient presents to an out-of-town physician requiring hydration and oxygen, which is determined to be caused by mountain sickness. How should this be coded?

_____

_____

Anesthesia and General Surgery

ANESTHESIA SERVICES

All anesthesia services are reported using the five-digit CPT code (00100–01999) plus the addition of a two-digit physical status modifier (P1–P6) to indicate the patient's state of health when undergoing the anesthesia. These modifiers are listed in the Anesthesia Guidelines of CPT. These codes include preoperative and postoperative visits by the anesthesiologist, care during the procedure, monitoring of vital signs, and any fluid administration. Anesthesia codes are assigned based upon the body site for the operation and not on the type of anesthesia administered.

When anesthesia services are provided under difficult circumstances, such as when the patient is of a particular age or faces unusual risks, a five-digit code must be added. This is referred to as qualifying circumstances, which is also located in the Anesthesia Guidelines of CPT.

CPT codes for moderate (conscious) sedation are listed in the Medicine section. CPT codes 99143 through 99150 are assigned for moderate (conscious) sedation with code selection based on age and intra-service time.

Name: _____   **Date:** _____

Coding Exercises

Exercise 1

Assign the CPT code for each of the following anesthesia services.

1. Water bath lithotripsy   _____
2. Amniocentesis   _____
3. Diagnostic arthroscopy of shoulder joint   _____
4. Anal fissurectomy   _____
5. Vaginal hysterectomy   _____
6. Corneal transplant   _____
7. Total hip arthroplasty   _____
8. Bilateral vasectomy   _____
9. Gastric bypass for morbid obesity   _____
10. Continuous epidural, labor, and delivery   _____

Exercise 2

Assign the CPT anesthesia code and the physical status modifier.

1. Blepharoplasty, patient with Type II diabetes, controlled   _____
2. Breast reduction, healthy patient, no complaints   _____
3. Needle biopsy of thyroid, hypertensive patient   _____
4. Amputation, ankle and foot, of a diabetic patient with gangrene and severe vascular disease   _____
5. Harrington rod procedure for scoliosis, healthy patient   _____
6. Transurethral resection of the prostate, hx. of CVA   _____
7. Heart/lung transplant, severe coronary artery disease   _____
8. Debridement of burn to hands and arms, 4% total body surface, of a diabetic patient   _____
9. Transvenous pacemaker insertion, sinus bradycardia   _____
10. Application of cast to lower leg, healthy patient   _____

CODING FOR ANESTHESIA AND GENERAL SURGERY—MODIFIERS

CPT standard modifiers may be used with anesthesia codes. These are as follows:

-22   *Unusual procedural service*—used with rare, unusual, or variable anesthesia services

-23   *Unusual anesthesia service*—applies when a general anesthesia is used in a procedure that requires either no anesthesia or local anesthesia

-32   *Mandated service*—used when a procedure is a mandated service, such as a PPO, third-party payor, governmental, legislative, or regulatory requirement

-47   *Anesthesia by surgeon*—used when regional or general anesthesia is provided by the surgeon, not for services performed by anesthesiologists or anesthetists, or those supervised by surgeons

-51   *Multiple procedures*—used to identify a second procedure or multiple procedures performed during the same operation

-53   *Discontinued procedure*—used when the procedure is discontinued after anesthesia has been administered but before the incision is made, due to extenuating circumstances or conditions that threaten the patient's health and well-being
       Note: Modifier -53 may not be used to report the elective cancellation of a procedure prior to administration of the patient's anesthesia and/or surgical preparation in the operating suite.

-59   *Distinct procedural service*—used to indicate that a procedure or service was distinct or independent from other non-E/M services performed on the same day

Coding Exercises

Assign the CPT code for the following anesthesia services. Assign any physical status or CPT modifiers, as well as add-on codes for qualifying circumstances.

1. Plastic repair for cleft lip, six-month-old infant   _____

2. Emergency appendectomy in 52-year-old, otherwise healthy female patient   _____

3. Bilateral orchiopexy in hypertensive patient, discontinued after anesthesia is induced due to severe hypertension   _____

4. Physiological support for harvesting organs from brain-dead patient for donor purposes   _____

5. Major abdominal vessel procedure for patient with severe arteriosclerotic cardiovascular disease, life-threatening   _____

6. Amputation of ankle and foot in an 85-year-old male, severely diabetic   _____

Certification Questions

Select or assign the proper CPT code.

1.   A 38-year-old female diagnosed with multiple sclerosis undergoes closed reduction of the right humerus.

   a. 01810-P2   c. 01830-P4

   b. 01820-P3   d. 01860-P2

2.   A laparoscopic cholecystectomy is performed on a 45-year-old with benign hypertension.

   a. 00700-P2   c. 00800-P2

   b. 00790-P2   d. 00840-P3

3.   A 32-year-old female with three children undergoes a tubal ligation. Her health is good.

   a. 00840-P1   c. 00851-P1

   b. 00848-P1   d. 00940-P1

4. A 78-year-old patient diagnosed with carcinoma of the prostate undergoes a transurethral resection of prostate (TURP).

    a. 00910-P3, 99100
    b. 00912-P3, 99100
    c. 00914-P3, 99100
    d. 00914-P4, 99100

5. A 59-year-old patient has a routine colonoscopy recommended at age 50 by his primary care physician. The gastroenterologist uses Versed IV for moderate conscious sedation for intraservice time of 45 minutes. What is the code for the anesthesia?

    a. 00810
    b. 45378
    c. 99144
    d. 99144, 99145

6. A 55-year-old female diagnosed with early rheumatoid arthritis undergoes anal fistulectomy.

    a. 00810-P2
    b. 00902-P2
    c. 00904-P2
    d. 01432-P3

7. A 16-year-old female with scoliosis undergoes insertion of Harrington rods. She is in good health otherwise.

    a. 00600-P1
    b. 00620-P1
    c. 00640-P1
    d. 00670-P1

8. Lesion removed from left upper thigh requiring regional IV administration of local anesthesia; patient has Type I diabetes mellitus.

    a. 00300-P2
    b. 00400-P2
    c. 01220-P2
    d. 01999-P2

Review Questions

1. Explain the purpose of assigning a physical status modifier.

    _____

2. List the three methods by which anesthesia can be administered.

    _____

    _____

    _____

3. List the three phases of anesthesia.

    _____

    _____

    _____

4. Describe the responsibilities of the anesthesiologist during the maintenance phase of anesthesia administration.

    _____

    _____

    _____

5. Codes are assigned from the _____ section of CPT for administering conscious sedation.

GENERAL SURGERY

General surgery refers to operations performed on the following body systems: respiratory, cardiovascular, hemic and lymphatic, mediastinum and diaphragm, digestive, urinary, male genital, female reproductive, endocrine, nervous, eye and ocular adnexa, and auditory.

Related types of procedures are grouped in CPT as follows:

- Incisions are procedures that involve cutting into a patient. These procedures generally end with -otomy or -tomy. Open surgical procedures are performed by creating a surgical incision to access the operative site.

- Excisions are procedures that involve surgical removal of something from the patient. These procedures generally end with -ectomy. Other terms used in this section include biopsy, resection, or removal.

- Introduction or removal procedures, such as amputation

- Repair/revision/reconstruction procedures, which generally end with -oorhaphy or -oplasty

- Manipulation or reduction, such as in fractures

- Fixation or fusion procedures, which generally end with -opexy

- Endoscopic or laparoscopic procedures, which generally end with -oscopy, such as colonoscopy, bronchoscopy, or arthroscopy

CPT CODING FOR GENERAL SURGERY

The following exercises are coded from the respiratory, digestive, urinary, male genital, endocrine, nervous, eye and ocular adnexa, and auditory systems. Exercises for the remaining systems are included in those chapters as related to the textbook.

Coding Exercises

Assign the CPT code for the following, using correct modifiers or add-on codes when indicated.

1. Glossectomy one-fourth portion of tongue _____

2. Repair of nasal septum _____

3. I&D of hematoma of epididymis _____

4. TURP _____

5. Removal of fecal impaction _____

6. Colonoscopy to control bleeding _____

7. Gastric bypass for morbid obesity _____

8. Exploration of bullet wound to chest _____

9. Ligation of internal hemorrhoids, single procedure _____

10. Intraocular lens exchange with ophthalmic endoscope _____ _____

11. Burr hole for drainage of intracranial abscess _____

12. Repair initial ventral hernia, reducible, with implantation of mesh _____ _____

13. Thoracentesis to remove fluid _____

14. Surgical decompression of carpal tunnel syndrome, left wrist   _____

15. Circumcision of newborn, clamp   _____

16. Removal of impacted cerumen, both ears   _____

17. Laparoscopic orchiectomy   _____

18. Nephrectomy, unilateral, open from living donor   _____

19. Cryotherapy of corneal lesion, left eye   _____

20. Total right lobectomy of liver   _____

21. Emergency endotracheal intubation   _____

22. Laparoscopic appendectomy   _____

23. Removal of bean from nose performed in urgent care center   _____

24. Cholecystectomy with appendectomy   _____

25. Control and packing of epistaxis, anterior   _____

ICD-9-CM CODING FOR GENERAL SURGERY

The following exercises are diagnoses, symptoms, or disorders related to the respiratory, digestive, urinary, male genital, endocrine, nervous, eye and ocular adnexa, and auditory systems. Exercises for the remaining systems are included in those chapters as related to the textbook.

Coding Exercises

Assign the ICD-9-CM code for the following exercises.

1. Crohn's disease   _____

2. Fecal impaction   _____

3. Foreign body in ear canal   _____

4. Deviation of nasal septum, acquired   _____

5. Gunshot wound to external chest   _____

6. Nosebleed   _____

7. Nystagmus   _____

8. Internal bleeding hemorrhoids   _____

9. Pleural effusion   _____

10. Carpal tunnel syndrome   _____

11. Impacted cerumen   _____

12. Acute appendicitis with peritonitis   _____

13. Chronic hepatitis Type B   _____

14. Testicular carcinoma   _____

15. Intracranial abscess   _____

16. Morbid obesity   _____

17. Hematoma of epididymis   _____

18. Urinary retention   _____

19. Carcinoma of tongue, posterior third   _____

20. Allergic rhinitis   _____

21. Acute bronchitis with bronchospasm   _____

22. Nontoxic thyroid goiter   _____

23. Cholelithiasis with cholecystitis   _____

24. Retinal hemorrhage   _____

25. Chronic serous otitis media   _____

Certification Questions

1. Blepharoplasty means surgical repair of the

   a. eyelid.

   b. forehead.

   c. nasal septum.

   d. mandible.

2. The insertion of tubes to create an artificial opening into the eardrum is a/an

   a. fenestration.

   b. sinusotomy.

   c. thoracostomy.

   d. tympanostomy.

3. Incision and drainage of the lacrimal gland is coded

   a. 68400.

   b. 68420.

   c. 68440.

   d. 68500.

4. The term cheiloplasty means surgical repair of the

   a. eyelid.

   b. forehead.

   c. lip.

   d. tongue.

5. A construction worker was seen in the Emergency Department for acute eye pain associated with a wood splinter entering the left eye. The patient is treated in the ED for repair of a corneal laceration with foreign body. The correct code is

   a. 65205.

   b. 65235.

   c. 65270.

   d. 65275.

6. A surgeon performs removal of external hemorrhoids by rubber band hemorrhoidectomy. The correct code is

   a. 46221.

   b. 46230.

   c. 46250.

   d. 46255.

7. A surgeon assists with a total abdominal hysterectomy with the Marshall-Marchetti-Krantz procedure. The correct code is

   a. 58150-80.

   b. 58152-80.

   c. 58200-80.

   d. 58267-80.

8. A surgeon performs circumcision of a 19-year-old male by surgical excision. The correct code is

    a. 54163.   c. 54161.

    b. 54160.   d. 54162.

9. A physician performs destruction of a rectal tumor by electrodessication. The correct code is

    a. 45190.   c. 45315.

    b. 45308.   d. 45320.

10. The surgeon performs a craniotomy to elevate a bone flap for subdural implantation of an electrode array for long-term monitoring of seizure activity. The correct code is

    a. 61526.   c. 61533.

    b. 61531.   d. 61566.

Review Questions

1. In order to describe a specific circumstance or an unusual event that alters the definition of the procedure, a coder would assign a(n)

    a. fifth digit.   c. add-on code.

    b. modifier.   d. E/M code.

2. The term manipulation or reduction refers to

    a. amputation.   c. fractures.

    b. catheters.   d. hemorrhage.

3. Which one of the following procedures requires the patient's age to be considered for assigning the appropriate CPT code?

    a. Gastric restrictive bypass   c. Tonsillectomy

    b. Intrauterine device insertion   d. Vasectomy

4. The procedure commonly performed to relieve angina is

    a. ERCP.   c. TURP.

    b. GIFT.   d. CABG.

5. Identify the endoscopic procedures and name the areas of the colon each examines.

    _____   _____

    _____   _____

    _____   _____

ICD-10-CM Coding

Code the following using ICD-10-CM.

1. A non-insulin-dependent patient with retinopathy and macular edema was referred to a retinal specialist for possible surgery.

    _____

2. A patient presents to his surgeon once again with hernia symptoms. The surgeon examines the patient and schedules immediate surgery once again to his right inguinal hernia.

    _____

3. A new patient is seen in the office for infection of the left great toenail. The patient also has Type I diabetes mellitus. An incision and drainage of the left great toenail are performed.

    _____

4. A patient undergoes a laparoscopic cholecystectomy for chronic cholecystitis.

    _____

5. A patient, age 36, has a rhinoplasty performed for a congenital nasal septum deformity.

    _____

Integumentary System

Chapter 7 discusses the integumentary system. This involves the body's skin, hair, and nails, including excision of skin lesions as well as burns and wound repair.

The integumentary is the largest organ system of the human body. Common coding services performed on this system are dedicated to conditions that often require destruction or removal. Coding of skin conditions from both a procedural and diagnostic perspective are important. Current diagnostic guidelines for skin conditions is fairly limited in ICD-9-CM, however expand into further depth within the ICD-10-CM coding system. Coders may find neoplasm coding challenging when interpreting from a pathology report. Provider clarification before assigning any malignancy diagnosis code to a patient for the first time is beneficial to assure accuracy.

Name: _____   **Date:** _____

CODING LACERATIONS

The size of a lesion or laceration is measured and coded in centimeters. Therefore, when the documentation notes the size in inches, this amount must be converted to centimeters.

   1 inch = 2.54 cm

Coding Exercises

Convert inches to centimeters in the following questions, then assign the correct CPT code.

1. Excision, 1-inch benign lesion, left leg   _____   _____

2. Excision, 1/2-inch malignant lesion, finger   _____   _____

3. Simple repair of a 2-inch laceration, right foot   _____   _____

4. Intermediate repair of a 5-inch laceration of back   _____   _____

5. Layer closure of a 3-inch wound of the neck   _____   _____

6. Repair of laceration, 2.0 cm, anterior 2/3 of tongue   _____   _____

Other codes for integumentary system:

7. Hair transplant, 21 punch grafts   _____

8. Simple blepharoplasty, right upper lid   _____

9. I&D hematoma, left hand   _____

10. Puncture aspiration, breast cyst, right breast   _____

11. Wound suture, 3/4-inch right hand, 1/2-inch left foot   _____

12. Excessive skin resection and lipectomy, right buttock   _____

13. Simple right shoulder biopsy, single skin lesion   _____

14. Excision of malignant 1/2-inch lesion, neck   _____

15. Debridement of subcutaneous tissue for infection of foreskin of penis   _____

CODING BURNS

Burns are coded by site, depth or degree, and/or percentage of the body burned.

Depth or degree:

First-degree burn   Superficial, involving the epidermis. Characterized by redness, hypersensitivity, and sometimes pain.

Second-degree burn   Partial thickness, involving the dermis and epidermis. Characterized by redness, blistering, edema, and pain.

Third-degree burn	Full thickness, involving all three areas of the skin. Sensory nerves are destroyed and all sensation to pinprick is lost in the burned area.
Fourth-degree burn	Deep necrosis; life-threatening. Causes charring of the skin to the bone (e.g., electrical burns).
Fifth-degree burn	Bone visibly damaged, probably requiring amputation.

Coding Exercises

Code the following from ICD-9-CM.

1. Second-degree burn, right upper arm and shoulder

_____ _____ _____

2. Third-degree burn, entire trunk, TBSA 35%

_____ _____

3. Burn of mouth, pharynx, and esophagus

_____ _____ _____

4. Blisters on back of hand

_____ _____ _____

5. Erythema on forearm and elbow

_____ _____ _____

6. First-degree burns of face and both eyes involving cornea, eyelids, nose, cheeks, and lips

_____ _____

7. Severe sunburn to arms and shoulders with blistering

_____

Certification Questions

Code the following exercises from ICD-9-CM as indicated.

1. In which procedure is foreign material or contaminated tissue removed from a wound, infected lesion, or trauma site in order to clean and expose the surrounding healthy tissue?

    a. Biopsy
    b. Cryosurgery
    c. Debridement
    d. Incision and drainage

2. When a decision for surgery is dependent upon the biopsy results during the same session, what modifier is also coded with the biopsy service?

    a. -25
    b. -57
    c. -58
    d. -59

3. A patient with Type II diabetes mellitus is treated for a decubitus ulcer, stage II of the sacral area, at a nursing facility.

    a. 250.70, 707.9
    b. 250.80, 707.03, 707.23
    c. 250.80, 707.03, 707.21
    d. 707.83, 707.22

4. A patient suffered a minor puncture injury to the finger when removing a staple at the office. Five days later he is treated for cellulitis of the finger with intravenous antibiotics.

    a. 681.00

    b. 681.02

    c. 682.4

    d. 682.9

5. A patient undergoes excision of an abscessed pilonidal cyst.

    a. 685.0, 11770

    b. 685.0, 11771

    c. 685.0, 11772

    d. 685.1, 11771

6. A patient is seen by a podiatrist for a "sore" on the right little toe. The "sore" is diagnosed as a hard corn deformity and undergoes paring of the lesion.

    a. 700, 11055

    b. 700, 11200

    c. 700, 11305

    d. 709.9, 11055

7. A patient is seen in the office for redness and irritation of the left eyelid. The diagnosis is contact dermatitis. The patient returns for recheck one week later and now has developed cellulitis to part of the area.

    a. 373.32, 373.13

    b. 373.32, 379.93

    c. 379.93, 373.13

    d. 379.93, 373.32, 373.13

8. Escharotomy is performed for a patient with a deep third-degree burn of the right foot with necrosis. The patient also has Type I adult onset diabetes mellitus, uncontrolled.

    a. 250.00, 945.32, 16035

    b. 250.03, 945.42, 948,00, 16035

    c. 250.03, 945.30, 16035

    d. 250.03, 945.52, 16035

9. A 15-year-old female receives a superficial burn to the forehead and cheeks from a tanning bed.

    a. 692.82, E926.2

    b. 692.71, E926.2

    c. 941.07, E926.3

    d. 941.17, E926.9

10. A patient is seen in the office by her primary care physician for removal of six skin tags on the back of her neck. During the procedure, she complains of feeling lightheaded. An expanded problem-focused history was performed. Chest is clear; cardio, no murmur; however, her heart is beating rapidly. Her blood pressure reveals an elevated reading of 182/96. She has no previous history of hypertension. The physician feels the elevation may be due to her anxiety about the procedure today. The BP will be checked weekly for the next month to monitor the readings. What codes are reported for this encounter?

    a. 11057, 99213-25

    b. 11200, 99213-25

    c. 11200, 99213-51

    d. 11200, 99214

Review Questions

1. Which depth of a burn involves all layers of the skin with destruction of nerve cells?

    a. First degree

    b. Second degree

    c. Third degree

    d. Fourth degree

2. Which burn is characterized by redness, hypersensitivity, and some pain?

    a. First degree

    b. Second degree

    c. Third degree

    d. Fourth degree

3.   Which one of the following would be classified as a fourth-degree burn?

   a. Blistering of skin due to burn to hand while cooking

   b. Erythema of face from exposure to steam

   c. Charring of skin to the bone with deep necrosis from contact with an electrical wire

   d. Destruction of sensory nerves from burn while extinguishing flames from a blanket

4.   List the organs/accessory organs included in the integumentary system.

   _____

   _____

   _____

5.   What is the purpose of the rule of nines?

   a. To calculate the percentage of total body surface affected in a burn patient

   b. To determine the depth or degree of the burn

   c. To determine if a lesion is benign or malignant

   d. To assist in conversion of the size of a wound

ICD-10-CM Coding

Assign ICD-10-CM codes for the following scenarios.

1.   Three common warts and two plantar warts were treated. What diagnosis codes should be used to report these conditions?

   _____

   _____

2.   After chemotherapy treatment was completed and no signs of cancer or reoccurrence of breast cancer was present, the patient elected to see the surgeon once again for reconstruction following her previous mastectomy. What ICD-10-CM code should the surgeon use for this encounter?

   _____

   _____

3.   A puncture wound was sustained to the patient's left hand while picking up a board with protruding nails, requiring a visit to his PCP. The wound was clean and free from any foreign body. What codes should be used for this encounter?

   _____

   _____

4.   A patient was diagnosed with a form of psoriasis known as "guttate." How should this be coded?

   _____

   _____

5.   A worried mother took her eight-year-old daughter, a frequent swimmer, to the pediatrician for a skin check. She was worried about potential melanoma on her face. The pediatrician diagnosed the young girl with freckles, which she determined to have been caused by the sun, and advised heavy use of sunscreen.

   _____

   _____

Orthopedics

Orthopedics is a medical specialty concerned with the prevention, investigation, diagnosis, and treatment of diseases, disorders, and injuries of the musculoskeletal system. This medical specialty is a major provider in the treatment of work-related injuries, motor vehicle accidents, and falls. In these instances, assigning E codes in addition to the diagnosis code will describe the cause of the injury in order to determine liability for the charges, such as workers' compensation, homeowner's insurance, or auto insurance.

Fractures involve the musculoskeletal system and are the result of a trauma or accident; however, there are also pathological fractures that occur in bones that are weakened by disease. They are usually spontaneous but sometimes occur in connection with a slight trauma that ordinarily would not result in a fracture in healthy bone. There are many underlying causes for pathological fractures, including osteoporosis, metastatic tumor of the bone, osteomyelitis, Paget's disease, disuse atrophy, hyperparathyroidism, and nutritional or congenital disorders.

Dislocation, also called luxation, is a disarrangement of two or more bones from their articular processes. An incomplete dislocation is called a subluxation. When a dislocation is associated with a fracture at the same location, code only the fracture. It is possible to have a fracture and dislocation of the same bone. When the fracture and dislocation have occurred at different sites, two codes can be assigned.

Name: _____   **Date:** _____

EXERCISES

Coding Exercises

Code the following conditions using Volumes 1 and 2 of ICD-9-CM.

1. Acute and chronic gouty arthritis   _____   _____
2. Chronic nodular rheumatoid arthritis w/polyneuropathy _____   _____
3. Herniated intervertebral disk, L4–5   _____
4. Chronic lumbosacral sprain   _____
5. Primary osteoarthritis of hip   _____
6. Osteomyelitis of left distal femur due to diabetes   _____   _____
7. Adhesive capsulitis, left shoulder   _____
8. Recurrent dislocation of patella   _____
9. Multiple compression fractures of vertebrae due to senile osteoporosis   _____   _____
10. Cervical spondylosis, C5–C6, C6–C7   _____
11. Fracture, right tibia, in person with AIDS   _____   _____
12. Fracture of left ilium in patient with Type II diabetes mellitus _____   _____
13. Greenstick fracture. third digit, right foot   _____
14. Multiple fractures, right femur, distal end   _____
15. Open fracture maxilla   _____

Coding Exercises

Code the following procedures from CPT.

1. Application of figure-of-eight cast   _____
2. Surgical exploration of gunshot wound to the chest with debridement and removal of the bullet   _____
3. Arthroscopy of shoulder with rotator cuff repair   _____
4. Aspiration of ganglion cyst of wrist   _____
5. Open treatment of clavicular fracture with internal fixation   _____
6. Arthroscopy, knee, surgical, for infection, lavage, and drainage   _____
7. Removal of nail from foot, deep   _____
8. Treatment of spontaneous hip dislocation by splint   _____
9. Amputation of metatarsal of great toe   _____

10. Excision of tumor of thigh, intramuscular, 3 cm   _____

11. Excision of benign tumor of the scapula with allograft   _____

12. Insertion of Harrington rod in patient with scoliosis, following posterior arthrodesis, eight vertebrae, no cast   _____   _____

13. Cartilage graft of the nasal septum   _____

14. Application of cranial halo of underdeveloped child   _____

15. Arthroscopy of elbow with limited debridement to remove gravel   _____

Certification Questions

1. A patient is seen and evaluated for osteoarthritis of the right knee. Aspiration of the knee revealed no fluid. The site was injected with 2 mL of hylan G-F 20 (Synvisc) without complication. The correct codes are

    a. 715.06, 20610.

    b. 715.96, 20605.

    c. 715.96, 20610.

    d. 716.96, 20610.

2. A patient diagnosed with Dupuytren's contracture of the left hand undergoes a palmar fasciotomy using open technique. The correct codes are

    a. 728.6, 26040-LT.

    b. 728.6, 26045-LT.

    c. 728.6, 26121-LT.

    d. 728.6, 26123-LT.

3. Which one of the following is an example of an open fracture?

    a. Comminuted

    b. Compound

    c. Greenstick

    d. Impacted

4. What are the two most common procedures associated with fractures?

    a. Incision and drainage

    b. Luxation and subluxation

    c. Open and closed

    d. Reduction and fixation

5. A 12-year-old boy is seen in the ED following a fall from his bicycle. An X-ray shows a closed fracture of the greater tuberosity of the left humerus. The correct codes are

    a. 812.03, E826.1.

    b. 812.09, E826.1.

    c. 812.13, E826.1.

    d. 812.20, E826.1.

6. A 75-year-old female is diagnosed with a pathological fracture of the hip secondary to Paget's disease. The correct code(s) is(are)

    a. 731.0.

    b. 731.0, 733.14.

    c. 733.14.

    d. 820.8.

7. A patient diagnosed with acquired trigger thumb undergoes tendon sheath incision release surgery. The correct codes are

    a. 26055, 727.03.

    b. 26055, 756.89.

    c. 26060, 756.89.

    d. 26160, 727.03.

8. Which one of the following is considered an autoimmune disease/disorder of the musculoskeletal system?

    a. Osteoarthritis   c. Schmorl's nodes

    b. Rheumatoid arthritis   d. Scoliosis

9. A new patient is seen in the office complaining of weakness of the right side of her face with some paralysis. Examination of the patient reveals a diagnosis of Bell's palsy. The patient's overall health is otherwise good. The correct codes are

    a. 99201, 351.0.   c. 99201, 780.79, 351.0.

    b. 99211, 351.0.   d. 99202, 780.79, 351.0.

10. A patient was initially seen in the office for recurrent ganglion cyst of the right wrist. Initial treatment had been an injection into the affected area. Today the cyst is surgically removed in the ambulatory surgical center. The correct codes are

    a. 25110, 727.43.   c. 25112, 727.43.

    b. 25111, 727.43.   d. 25112, 727.49.

Review Questions

1. List some of the diseases, disorders, and injuries treated by an orthopedic practice.

    _____

    _____

    _____

2. Name three diseases/disorders that may cause a pathological fracture.

    _____

    _____

    _____

3. An "open" fracture means the skin is broken. What five descriptive terms are listed in ICD-9-CM to define an open fracture?

    _____

    _____

    _____

    _____

4. A "closed" fracture means the skin is not broken through and bone is not protruding. What seven descriptive terms are listed in ICD-9-CM to define a closed fracture?

    _____

    _____

    _____

5. What incidents may require assigning an E code to the diagnosis code?

    _____

    _____

ICD-10-CM Coding

Assign ICD-10-CM codes for the following scenarios.

1. After sustaining a fall down the stairs at her apartment, the patient was rushed to the Emergency Department where multiple rib fractures were treated on her right side.

    _____ _____ _____

2. A patient with osteochondritis dissecans of the right shoulder was seen in follow-up by her orthopedic surgeon.

    _____

3. A new patient was seen by the rheumatologist for evaluation and treatment of her recently diagnosed rheumatoid arthritis.

    _____

4. A worker is injured in a fall from a ladder while working on a roof at a private residence, resulting in a fractured pelvic bone.

    _____

5. A 75-year-old female is diagnosed with a pathological fracture of the hip secondary to Paget's disease.

    _____

Cardiology and the Cardiovascular System

9

The cardiovascular system encompasses the heart and vessels. Specialists in the diagnosis and treatment of the heart include the cardiologist (the physician specializing in cardiology) and the cardiothoracic surgeon (one who specializes in surgical procedures of the heart and chest). Other physicians utilize codes and procedures related to cardiology, such as electrocardiograms, CPR, and other therapeutic services. Conditions treated by many physicians, such as hypertension and hypercholesterolemia, involve the cardiovascular system.

Knowledge of the anatomical structure and the function of the heart is essential to coding cardiac procedures and disorders. Understanding the terminology of the heart is important, including the terminology's abbreviations and acronyms.

Name: _____   **Date:** _____

EXERCISES

Coding Exercises

Code the following diagnoses, symptoms, and disorders from ICD-9-CM.

1. Angina pectoris with benign hypertension   _____   _____
2. Atrial fibrillation   _____
3. Mitral valve insufficiency, congenital   _____
4. AMI inferoposterior wall, initial   _____
5. Abdominal aortic aneurysm   _____
6. Chest pain, R/O AMI   _____
7. Family hx. of ischemic heart disease   _____
8. Hypertensive heart disease   _____
9. CHF with atrial fibrillation   _____   _____
10. Chronic rheumatic pericarditis   _____

Coding Exercises

Code the following procedures and services from CPT.

1. Insertion of dual chamber pacemaker   _____
2. Routine venipuncture   _____
3. Electrocardiogram, 12 leads, with interpretation/report   _____
4. Postop hemorrhage of chest, exploration   _____
5. Pericardiotomy to remove blood clot   _____
6. Pulmonary valve replacement   _____
7. 2D transthoracic echocardiography with treadmill with Cardiolyte for stress induction, complete   _____   _____
8. Insertion and placement of Swan-Ganz catheter for monitoring   _____
9. Heart-lung transplant with recipient cardiectomy/pneumonectomy   _____
10. Transluminal balloon angioplasty, aortic vessel   _____

Certification Questions

1. A 45-year-old male is admitted to the coronary unit with acute MI of the inferoposterior wall, initial, with congestive heart failure and hypertension. The ICD-9-CM codes for this admission are

   a. 410.21, 428.0, 401.9.

   b. 410.30, 428.0, 401.9.

   c. 410.31, 428.0, 401.9.

   d. 410.41, 428.0, 401.9.

2. A 32-year-old patient is in the office with the complaint of a fast, racing heart rate. The EKG performed in the office and read by the physician shows premature ventricular contractions. The patient was last seen by this physician four years ago when treated for hypertension. Blood pressure today is elevated at 192/94. Patient states he has taken the antihypertensive medication sporadically for the past four years. This is coded

   a. 99203, 93000, 427.69, 401.9.

   b. 99203, 93000, 427.69, 401.0.

   c. 99213, 93000, 427.69, 401.9.

   d. 99213, 93000, 427.69, 401.0.

3. The patient in question 2 is referred to a cardiologist for consultation, evaluation, and treatment recommendations for the PVCs. An EKG is performed that again shows the PVCs. The patient will be monitored for 24 hours by a Holter monitor producing a full printout, recording, analysis, report, physician review, and interpretation. This is coded

   a. 99204, 93000, 93224.

   b. 99243, 93000, 93224.

   c. 99253, 93000, 93224.

   d. 99263, 93000, 93224.

4. Tachycardia means

   a. cardiac insufficiency.

   b. fast heart rate.

   c. irregular heart rate.

   d. slow heart rate.

5. A 39-year-old female is referred to a cardiologist with a diagnosis of mitral valve prolapse. A cardiac stress test done previously at the hospital is reviewed and interpreted by the cardiologist during the consultation visit in the office. Her health has been good otherwise. This is coded

   a. 99203, 93015, 424.0.

   b. 99242, 93015, 424.0.

   c. 99242, 93018, 424.0.

   d. 99262, 93018, 424.0.

6. A 49-year-old male was seen in the Emergency Department for chest pain. He had been seen in the hospital three months ago for a myocardial infarction. This is coded

   a. 410.92.

   b. 786.50, 411.1.

   c. 785.50, 414.8.

   d. 414.8.

7. A patient complains of difficulty breathing and shortness of air with exertion. The physician notes the patient has severe edema in the lower extremities. She is hypertensive with an elevated blood pressure reading today. Diagnoses documented for today's visit are congestive heart failure and hypertension. This is coded

   a. 398.91.

   b. 402.91.

   c. 428.0, 401.9.

   d. 786.05, 782.3, 401.9.

8. A patient is admitted to the cardiac unit with acute MI, initial, of the inferolateral wall and a third-degree AV block. This is coded

   a. 410.20, 426.0.

   b. 410.21, 426.0.

   c. 410.21, 426.6.

   d. 410.21, 426.10.

9. A patient undergoes repair of a thoracoabdominal aortic aneurysm with graft and cardiopulmonary bypass. This is coded

   a. 33860, 441.7.

   b. 33877, 441.4.

   c. 33877, 441.7.

   d. 33877, 441.03.

10. A patient is admitted to the hospital with bronchopneumonia and sick sinus syndrome on May 3, 2011, and is followed daily by this physician until discharged on May 6, 2011. The physician spent 50 minutes on discharge services, which included new medications prescribed, review of previous medications to be continued at home, and follow-up chest X-ray in one week before returning to the office for recheck. What are the codes reported for physician billing during the hospitalization?

    a. 99218, 99224 x 2, 99217, 485, 427.81

    b. 99221, 99231 x 2, 99239, 485, 427.81

    c. 99221, 99232 x 2, 99238, 486, 427.8.

    d. 99231, 99232 x 2, 99239, 485, 427.89

Review Questions

Identify each of the following cardiac acronyms.

1. CABG _____

2. BBB _____

3. PAD _____

4. MVP _____

5. PTCA _____

6. ASHD _____

7. HTN _____

8. CHF _____

9. CAD _____

10. CPR _____

Match each of the following terms with the correct definition.

_____	1. Atrium	A. Blood flow obstruction
_____	2. Ventricles	B. Middle layer of heart
_____	3. Tricuspid	C. Outside covering of heart
_____	4. Bicuspid	D. Lower chambers of heart
_____	5. SA node	E. Upper chambers of heart
_____	6. Myocardium	F. Conductor for electrical impulses

_____	7. Pericardium	G.	AV valves
_____	8. Endocardium	H.	Natural pacemaker of heart
_____	9. Bundle of His	I.	Mitral valves
_____	10. Occlusion	J.	Innermost layer of heart

ICD-10-CM Coding

Assign ICD-10-CM codes for the following scenarios.

1. Medication refill was provided for an 86-year-old patient seen on follow-up for her hypertension.

   _____

2. The MRI results confirmed a recent cerebral infarction, which was determined to have been caused by a right cerebellar artery thrombosis.

   _____

3. A 68-year-old patient is admitted to CCU for evaluation of an acute myocardial infarction.

   _____

4. The patient is admitted for placement of a permanent pacemaker, AV sequential, for trifascicular heart block.

   _____

5. The patient, age 81 years, is seen in the ED for congestive heart failure.

   _____

OB/GYN

10

FEMALE GENITAL SYSTEM: MATERNITY CARE AND DELIVERY

The following subsection of CPT-4 covers procedures performed on the female genital system. It also addresses maternity care and delivery. In the female genital system, codes for body site and for in vitro fertilization are listed by the type of procedure. Note that in some descriptors, the terms salpingo- and oophor- are used, and in others, tube(s) and ovary(s). For example, the term salpingo-oophorectomy has the same meaning as removal of the ovary and its fallopian tube.

The maternity care and delivery codes have a unique organization. They are grouped as follows: antepartum services; excision; introduction; repair; vaginal delivery, antepartum, and postpartum care (normal uncomplicated cases); cesarean delivery; delivery after previous cesarean delivery; abortion; and other procedures.

Name: _____   **Date:** _____

THE OBSTETRIC PACKAGE

The guidelines for maternity care/delivery describe the obstetric package of services normally provided for uncomplicated cases. The package consists of antepartum care, delivery, and postpartum care, as described. Before coding obstetrical services, one should study these notes carefully to avoid unbundling. Understanding the obstetric package also helps the coder correctly report those services that are not part of the package and that can be coded separately.

Coding Exercises

Code the following procedures from CPT.

1. Complete radical vulvectomy   _____
2. D&C, postpartum hemorrhage   _____
3. Total abdominal hysterectomy   _____
4. Subtotal hysterectomy   _____
5. Insertion of IUD   _____
6. Diagnostic hysteroscopy   _____
7. Bilateral complete salpingo-oophorectomy   _____
8. Radical abdominal hysterectomy w/salpingo-oophorectomy   _____
9. Vaginectomy and complete removal of vaginal wall   _____
10. Routine obstetric care/vaginal delivery   _____
11. Episiotomy by assisting physician   _____
12. Miscarriage surgically completed in first trimester _____
13. Chromotubation of oviduct including materials   _____   _____
14. Five visits for antepartum care only   _____
15. Bilateral drainage of ovarian cysts by abdominal approach   _____

COMPLICATIONS OF PREGNANCY, CHILDBIRTH, AND PUERPERIUM

Codes in this chapter of ICD-9-CM classify conditions that are involved with pregnancy, childbirth, and puerperium. Many categories require a fifth-digit subclassification based on when the complications occur (referred to as the episode of care), either before birth (antepartum), during birth, or after birth (postpartum).

These codes are assigned to the conditions of the mother only, not of the infant. They cover the course of pregnancy and childbirth from conception through the puerperium, which is the six-week period following delivery.

Coding Exercises

Code the following from Volumes 1 and 2 of ICD-9-CM.

1. Ectopic pregnancy, w/o intrauterine pregnancy _____
2. Incomplete spontaneous abortion w/complications _____
3. Hemorrhage in pregnancy at 18 weeks _____
4. False labor _____
5. Essential hypertension complicating pregnancy _____
6. Gestational diabetes _____
7. Delivery of triplets _____ _____
8. Uterine death of delivered late-term fetus _____
9. Rh incompatibility _____
10. Nipple fissure in fourth week after childbirth _____
11. Normal delivery of single liveborn _____ _____
12. Normal delivery of liveborn twins _____ _____
13. Normal delivery of quadruplets, three liveborn, one stillborn _____ _____

CONDITIONS ORIGINATING IN THE PERINATAL PERIOD

Using ICD-9-CM, code the following conditions of the fetus or newborn infant (neonate), which covers the perinatal period (the period shortly before birth until 28 days following delivery). The codes used for the hospitalization that results in the birth are secondary to codes from categories V30 through V39. Note the use of the fourth digit to designate the birth location and of the fifth digit to specify hospital births.

Coding Exercises

1. Fetal alcohol syndrome _____
2. Fetus affected by mother's malnutrition _____
3. Neonatal hepatitis _____
4. Respiratory distress syndrome _____
5. Convulsions in newborn _____
6. Hospital birth of living infant, premature, weighs 2,000 grams _____
7. Full-term birth in hospital of living male child, delivered by cesarean section, w/neonatal transient hyperthyroidism _____ _____
8. Premature birth of female twins, first child delivered in ambulance en route to hospital, second child delivered in hospital _____ _____ _____

Certification Questions

1. A pregnant patient is treated for an acute urinary tract infection due to *E. coli* bacteria.
    a. 646.50, 599.0, 041.4
    b. 646.60, 599.0, 041.4
    c. 646.61, 599.0, 041.4
    d. 646.63, 599.0, 041.4

2. A pregnant woman is admitted to the hospital for vaginal bleeding following a fall at home. She is at 20 weeks gestation.
    a. 640.01, 641.83, E885.9
    b. 646.30, 641.90, E849.0
    c. 641.93, 640.03, E880.9, E849.0
    d. 640.03, 666.0, E884.2

3. A woman in her 22nd week of pregnancy is evaluated by her OB for excessive vomiting caused by acute gastroenteritis.
    a. 643.23, 558.41
    b. 643.80, 558.9
    c. 643.83, 558.9
    d. 643.93, 558.9

4. The physician successfully performs resuscitation on a newborn infant with cardiac distress during delivery.
    a. 99461
    b. 99463
    c. 99464
    d. 99465

5. A patient consults a surgeon for an opinion on a recommended hysterectomy in the office setting by her primary care physician. This visit is coded using what code range?
    a. 99201–99205
    b. 99241–99245
    c. 99251–99255
    d. 99281–99285

6. A 33-year-old patient is seen for an annual pelvic examination including Pap smear. She is complaining of menorrhagia since her last exam one year ago. Pelvic exam is normal. A CBC performed in the office today reveals iron deficiency anemia.
    a. V72.31, 626.2, 280.9
    b. V76.2, 626.2, 280.9
    c. V721.31, 626.2, 281.9
    d. V76.2, 626.2, 281.9

7. A 39-year-old female undergoes a vaginal hysterectomy with the Marshall-Marchetti-Krantz procedure; uterus weighs 255 grams.
    a. 58267
    b. 58270
    c. 58290
    d. 58293

8. Patient is seen for excision of Bartholin's cyst.
    a. 56420
    b. 56440
    c. 56740
    d. 57135

9. Patient receives tubal ligation, vaginal approach, bilateral, for sterilization purposes.
    a. 58600, V26.51
    b. 58605, V26.51
    c. 58600-50, V25.2
    d. 58605-50, V26.51

10. When coding and billing for obstetrical services in a normal, uncomplicated pregnancy, a global package concept is used, which includes

a. antepartum, delivery, and postpartum care.

b. Pap smear, prenatal panel, delivery.

c. pregnancy test, antepartum and postpartum care.

d. pregnancy test, monthly exams, delivery.

Review Questions

1. The term gestation means

a. the duration of pregnancy.

b. the completion of delivery.

c. the beginning of the menstrual function.

2. The obstetric package for uncomplicated pregnancy and delivery includes three services. They are

_____

_____

_____

3. The term puerperium refers to

a. the period of time before delivery.

b. the period of time after delivery.

c. the recovery time after delivery for the uterus to return to normal.

d. the beginning of menstrual function.

4. Name four of the internal organs of the female reproductive system.

_____

_____

_____

_____

5. List four sexually transmitted diseases.

_____

_____

_____

_____

ICD-10-CM Coding

Assign ICD-10-CM codes for the following scenarios.

1. A patient in her second trimester was encouraged by her PCP to seek assistance from an OB/GYN provider to supervise her pregnancy, which she has kept hidden from her family. He stressed the importance of proper antenatal care and the direct impact it has on a positive outcome. What ICD-10-CM code should the OB/GYN provider use to monitor this patient?

_____

_____

2. A 32-year-old female required a return trip to her physician's office for another Pap smear because her previous Pap smear was unsatisfactory and lacked enough cells to run the test. What should the return diagnosis be coded for the repeat Pap smear?

    _____

    _____

3. What ICD-10-CM code should be used for a patient returning for follow-up of her gestational diabetes, which is currently under control by dietary measures?

    _____

    _____

4. A third-degree perineal laceration was sustained during delivery and required extensive repair. What ICD-10-CM code should be used to report the laceration?

    _____

    _____

5. A healthy newborn by vaginal delivery occurred at 39.5 weeks gestation without any complication. Code this delivery.

    _____

    _____

Radiology, Pathology, and Laboratory

RADIOLOGY

The Radiology section of CPT contains five categories of services:

- *Diagnostic imaging or X-rays* include CAT/CT scans, MRI, mammography, and angiography.

- *Diagnostic ultrasound* uses sound waves to create an image: A-mode, M-mode, B-scan, and real-time.

- *Radiation oncology* uses radiation: measured in rads, based on number of areas, ports, and blocks. Radiation materials implanted directly into an anatomical site using ribbons and sources is called brachytherapy, which is often used in the treatment of breast cancer.

- *Nuclear medicine* uses radioactive materials within the body to diagnose or use in therapeutic testing, such as a stress test.

- *Interventional radiology* is a combination of both a surgical procedure and a radiological service.

Radiology CPT codes are used when radiological services are performed by the physician or by someone under the supervision of a physician. A modifier or specified code referred to as the professional component of the service may be assigned if the radiological service was not performed by the physician but was read and interpreted by the physician. Modifier -26 is used to indicate the physician provided the professional portion of the test only; modifier -TC is used to indicate that only the technical component was provided. When the CPT code includes "supervision and interpretation," it cannot be used for providing the technical portion of the test.

Name: _____   **Date:** _____

Coding Exercises

Assign the correct CPT code to the following exercises.

1. Bilateral bronchogram   _____

2. Chest X-ray, anterior and lateral   _____

3. GI series with small bowel and air studies, without KUB   _____

4. Initial screening mammogram, bilateral   _____

5. Cervical MRI, no contrast   _____

6. Complete obstetrical B-scan, first trimester   _____

7. Bilateral carotid angiogram, supervision/interpretation   _____

8. DXA scan for bone density of hips, pelvis, spine   _____

9. X-ray for TMJ, right   _____

10. X-ray tibia and fibula, left leg, two views   _____

Certification Questions

1. A patient has a complete chest X-ray, four views, to recheck the status of bronchopneumonia.

   a. 71010   c. 71030

   b. 71020   d. 71035

2. A patient with a complaint of diarrhea alternating with constipation has a barium enema with air contrast of the colon.

   a. 74246   c. 74280

   b. 74270   d. 74283

3. A patient undergoes cardiac MRI for morphology and function without contrast material, including velocity flow mapping.

   a. 75557   c. 75561, 75565

   b. 75561   d. 75557, 75565

4. A 56-year-old female has her annual routine mammogram on October 5. After the films are reviewed, a small nodule is noted in the left breast. On October 21, a repeat mammogram is performed with a computer-aided detection image study of the left breast. What codes would be assigned for the procedures done on October 21?

   a. 77055-LT, 77051-LT   c. 77056-LT, 77051-LT

   b. 77055-LT, 77052-LT   d. 77057-LT, 77052-LT

5. An ultrasound of the neck is performed to check a diagnosis of hypothyroidism.

   a. 76536   **c.** 78006

   b. 78000   **d.** 78010

6. A patient diagnosed with gastroparesis has a gastric emptying study.

   a. 78261   **c.** 78264

   b. 78262   **d.** 78299

7. PET scan for tumor imaging of the chest is performed.

   a. 71550   **c.** 78811

   b. 78580   **d.** 78814

8. An ultrasound is performed on a 44-year-old female to check for ovarian cysts. The patient is not pregnant.

   a. 76801   **c.** 76830

   b. 76805   **d.** 76856

9. A patient has symptoms of temporomandibular joint disorder. X-ray is made, open and closed views, bilateral.

   a. 70328   **c.** 70332

   b. 70330   **d.** 70336

10. The driver of a motorcycle involved in an MVA is seen in the Emergency Department for evaluation and X-ray for possible fracture of the tibia and fibula.

    a. 73590   **c.** 73700

    b. 73592   **d.** 73706

Review Questions

1. Name the four categories of radiology coding located in the CPT code book.

   _____

   _____

   _____

   _____

2. What does each of the following abbreviations represent?

   MRI _____

   CT _____

   CAT _____

   PET _____

3. What is modifier -26 used to report?

   _____

4. Match the area or anatomical site with the correct nuclear medicine scan.

    _____ Osteomyelitis   A. Bone scan

    _____ Kidney function   B. Cardiac scan

    _____ Myocardial infarction   C. Lung scan

    _____ COPD   D. Renal scan

    _____ Ventricular aneurysms

    _____ Osteoporosis

5. Brachytherapy is used in the treatment of what type of carcinoma?

    _____

PATHOLOGY/LABORATORY

The Pathology/Laboratory section of CPT includes such topics as ordering the test, obtaining and pre-paring a specimen, following the testing process, and interpreting results. It is important to know where the service is performed when assigning the code. For example, a patient may be seen in the office for an annual Pap smear, where the specimen is obtained but sent to pathology for interpretation. The physician's office may be able to bill the collection of the specimen for preparation to be sent to the lab, but the outside source would bill for the testing and interpretation of the specimen, assigning a code from the Pathology section of CPT. As another example, a venipuncture code can be assigned for drawing blood in the office, but if the blood is sent to a lab for testing and reporting, the outside source would bill the patient for this service using laboratory codes from CPT.

Coding Exercises

Assign CPT codes to the following exercises.

1. Urinalysis dipstick, nonautomated, complete, with microscope   _____

2. Heavy metal screen   _____

3. Urine pregnancy test   _____

4. Electrolyte panel   _____

5. Fasting glucose, blood, quantitative   _____

6. Thyroid stimulating hormone   _____

7. Routine prothrombin time   _____

8. Autopsy as ordered by coroner   _____

9. Pap smear, vaginal/cervical slides, manual, under physician screening   _____

10. Stool test for *Helicobacter pylori*   _____

Certification Questions

1. A 49-year-old patient is seen in the office for a six-month evaluation of hyperlipidemia. The physician orders blood drawn in the office to be sent to the laboratory to check serum cholesterol, lipoprotein with HDL, and triglycerides. What codes would be assigned for physician billing?

    a. 99212, 36415   c. 99396, 36415

    b. 99212, 36415, 80061   d. 99396, 36415, 80061

2. A 19-year-old patient is seen in the office for ABO blood typing and a urine pregnancy test. She is an established patient in the practice. What codes would be assigned?

    a. 99202, 86900, 81025
    b. 99212, 86900, 81025
    c. 99212, 86910, 81025
    d. 99212, 86910, 81005

3. A physician orders a comprehensive metabolic panel. In addition, the order includes a CBC and TSH. How would this be coded?

    a. Code the comprehensive metabolic panel and the CBC and TSH individually.
    b. Code a general health panel.
    c. Code a basic metabolic panel and the CBC and TSH individually.
    d. Code a comprehensive metabolic panel.

4. A 69-year-old male has blood drawn in the lab for a Lee and White coagulation study to check the level for adjustment of his Coumadin dosage. This is coded

    a. 85300.
    b. 85337.
    c. 85345.
    d. 85348.

5. A 32-year-old female is seen in the office for her annual pelvic examination with Pap smear. She is a new patient to this office and states she is in good health and has no complaints today. A specimen is obtained for the Pap smear and sent to the laboratory. She will be notified of the results in 10 days. She will return prn. How is this coded for physician billing?

    a. 88147
    b. 88150
    c. 99201
    d. 99385

6. What is the code for a urine culture with quantitative colony count for bacteria?

    a. 87081
    b. 87084
    c. 87086
    d. 87088

7. A patient is seen in the laboratory for a three-hour glucose tolerance test. This is coded

    a. 82946.
    b. 82947.
    c. 82951.
    d. 82952.

8. A specimen is received by the laboratory for a semen analysis to check volume, presence, count, and motility of sperm, as well as differential. This is coded

    a. 89300.
    b. 89310.
    c. 89320.
    d. 89321.

9. A blood specimen is received by the laboratory for a creatinine test. This is coded

    a. 82540.
    b. 82550.
    c. 82565.
    d. 82570.

10. A patient who is hospitalized has blood drawn for testing of blood gases, including calculated O_2 saturation. This is coded

    a. 82800.
    b. 82803.
    c. 82805.
    d. 82810.

Review Questions

1. What does the term pathology mean?

    _____

    _____

    _____

    _____

2. Name five tests that are designated as waived laboratory tests as defined by CLIA '88 regulations.

    _____

    _____

    _____

    _____

    _____

3. How does a venipuncture code differ from any other collection of specimen code?

    _____

    _____

    _____

4. List the tests included in the electrolyte panel.

    _____

    _____

    _____

5. What does each of the following laboratory abbreviations represent?

    BUN   _____

    CBC   _____

    TSH   _____

    PSA   _____

    3-hr GTT   _____

    FBS   _____

ICD-10-CM Coding

Assign ICD-10-CM codes for the following scenarios.

1. A patient on long-term use of Lipitor for hypercholesterolemia has a six-month check of his lipid panel.

   _____

2. A 36-year-old female has routine bilateral screening mammography for fibrocystic disease of the right breast.

   _____

3. A patient diagnosed with hemophilia A has routine bleeding and clotting tests.

   _____

Medicine

The Medicine section of CPT contains codes for a variety of procedures and services provided by many different types of health care providers. Two basic types of subsections are included: those that are procedure related and those that refer to particular medical specialties, such as physical medicine, ophthalmology, and home health services.

The Medicine section includes special services, procedures, and reports. These provide codes for miscellaneous services that are an adjunct to the basic services rendered to indicate the special circumstances under which a basic procedure is performed, such as specimen handling, special insurance reporting forms, and supplies and materials. Always code documented services and procedures that are provided or performed by a physician. While there are codes for these special circumstances, third-party payers do not always reimburse the provider.

Name: _____   **Date:** _____

EXERCISES

Coding Exercises

Assign CPT codes to the following.

1. Medical testimony   _____

2. MMR, live vaccine, SQ, age six   _____ _____

3. Administration code for PCN, IM   _____

4. Percutaneous allergy testing by puncture with allergenic extracts, immediate type reaction, 14 tests   _____

5. Color vision exam, for color-blindness   _____

6. Psychotherapy including patient and family   _____

7. Tympanometry   _____

8. Medical hypnotherapy to stop smoking   _____

9. CPAP   _____

10. Oral polio virus vaccine and administration   _____ _____

11. Rabies immune globulins, IM, age 10   _____ _____

12. Cardiovascular stress test, treadmill, complete   _____

13. Spirometry for pulmonary function analysis   _____

14. Completion of insurance claim forms for life insurance application/questionnaire   _____

15. Laser treatment for psoriasis, 375 sq cm   _____

Certification Questions

1. Gastroesophageal reflux test including placement, recording, analysis, and interpretation for patient suspected of GERD.

   a. 91010
   b. 91020
   c. 91034
   d. 91037

2. A new patient, age 55, is seen in the office for an expanded problem-focused exam, detailed history, and low-complexity decision making. He also receives pneumococcal and flu vaccines given IM.

   a. 90471, 90472, 90658, 90732
   b. 90471, 90658, 90732, 99202
   c. 90471, 90472, 90658, 90732, 99202
   d. 90471, 90472, 90655, 90732, 99202

3. A patient is given IV hydration for 100 minutes along with an IV push of 20 mg of compazine to relieve her nausea and vomiting.

    a. 96360, 96361, 96374 J0780 x 2   c. 99365 x 2, J0780 x 20
    b. 96372, 96374, J0780 x 2   d. 96360 x 2, J0780 x 20

4. A patient receives assistance in her home for bathing, dressing, and meal preparation.

    a. 99348   c. 99509
    b. 99347   d. 99600

5. A patient removed from life support is evaluated by EEG for cerebral death.

    a. 95830   c. 95822
    b. 95812   d. 95824

6. An established patient returns for a routine eye examination on an intermediate level. He has decided to continue with contact lenses, and the ophthalmologist supervises the fitting and adaptation of the lenses. The patient receives a 90-day supply of the prescribed contact lenses.

    a. 92002, 92310   c. 92012, 92325
    b. 92012, 92310   d. 92012, 92314

7. Referring to question 6, the patient calls three months later to state he has lost his right contact lens. The office orders a replacement lens for the patient to pick up at the office.

    a. 92310-52   c. 92326
    b. 92311   d. 92325

8. An established patient is seen in the office for a follow-up EKG after being seen in the hospital Emergency Department for chest pain. A 12-lead study is performed, including interpretation and report by the physician. The exam is expanded problem-focused and the decision making, low complexity.

    a. 99203, 93000   c. 99213, 93010
    b. 99213, 93000   d. 99282, 93244

9. Five patients participating in a group psychotherapy session receive audiotapes provided by the physician.

    a. 90806, 99071   c. 90853, 99071
    b. 90846, 99070   d. 90901, 99070

10. A patient is seen in the office for chemotherapy administration by intra-arterial push technique, performed on a monthly basis.

    a. 96409, 99213   c. 96411, 99212
    b. 96420   d. 96420, 99213

Review Questions

1. Which one of the following services would be assigned a code from the Medicine section of CPT?

    a. Hospital admission   c. Interpretation of radiology report
    b. Immunizations   d. Nursing facility service

2. Name five subsections located in the Medicine section of CPT.

    _____

    _____

    _____

    _____

    _____

3. In what subsection of the Medicine section would you locate codes for polysomnography and sleep studies?

    a. Allergy

    b. Endocrinology

    c. Neurology

    d. Physical Medicine and Rehabilitation

4. Which one of the following medications is an IM antibiotic injection?

    a. Diazepam

    b. Phenergen

    c. Vitamin B-12

    d. Zithromax

5. When coding an immunization, which of the following is correct?

    a. An administration code is assigned in addition to the vaccine code.

    b. An administration code is assigned in addition to the prophylactic code.

    c. An administration code, prophylactic code, and HCPCS codes are assigned.

    d. None of the above.

6. Forty-five minutes of individual intervention measures for a 12-year-old patient with cystic fibrosis are required in order for her medical treatment to be successful. How should this be coded?

    a. 96152 x 3

    b. 96154

    c. 90806

    d. 96152

ICD-10-CM Coding

Assign ICD-10-CM codes for the following scenarios.

1. After careful review of the sleep study results, it was determined that the patient was suffering from sleep deprivation and not sleep apnea. Instruction on work and lifestyle changes were given. Code this service.

    _____

2. A patient decides to visit the hand surgeon for an opinion following failed therapy for her carpal tunnel syndrome of her right arm. Code this service.

    _____

3. A dietician's services were requested to assist the patient with ongoing, chronic nutritional anemia. What diagnosis code should be reported for this condition?

    _____

4. A seven-year-old presented to the speech therapist for treatment of her newly diagnosed stuttering problem. How should the therapist report this diagnosis?

    _____

5. A patient pulled over for unsafe driving was thought to have been drinking. The county hospital performed a blood test, which confirmed the suspicion. How should this be coded?

    _____

Modifiers: A Practical Understanding

13

Nowadays, modifiers are a necessity in everyday coding. They paint a clearer picture of the services provided and offer a way to change or alter the service without compromising the procedural code foundation and intent. Used as a vehicle to assist in describing performed services correctly, these two-digit numeric or alphanumeric characters are critical to accurate reporting. Some modifiers are considered informational only (i.e., -RT for right or -LT for left), whereas others may have a direct impact on reimbursement (i.e., -52 Reduced services). Modifiers are found in both CPT and HCPCS Level II (HCPCSII) and must be used judiciously when applicable. This information often weighs heavily on whether or not the provider gets the correct payment or any payment at all. There are approximately 35 CPT modifiers and over 200 HCPCSII modifiers available. Certain CPT and HCPCSII modifiers are used very frequently, and others are used very rarely. This is especially true for HCPCSII modifiers, as administrative rules and coverage change frequently and may require specific information to be reported (i.e., modifier HYFunded by a Juvenile Justice Agency).

It is not unusual to append HCPCSII modifiers to CPT codes when correct coding warrants the application or, on rarer occasions, to append CPT modifiers to HCPCII codes.

Name: _____   **Date:** _____

EXERCISES

Coding Exercises

Match the following modifiers with their usage.

1. _____ E/M service in postop period   A. -54
2. _____ Anesthesia by surgeon   B. -90
3. _____ Assistant surgeon   C. -53
4. _____ Bilateral procedure   D. -24
5. _____ Reduced services   E. -91
6. _____ Professional service only   F. -58
7. _____ Surgical care only   G. -52
8. _____ Discontinued procedure   H. -50
9. _____ Reference laboratory   I. -26
10. _____ Repeat laboratory test   J. -80
11. _____ Staged procedure   K. -47

Complete the following coding scenarios by identifying the appropriate CPT and applicable modifiers.

1. A 65-year-old female underwent an open, debulking procedure to remove extensive abdominal tumors. During this procedure, the surgeon felt an appendectomy was warranted and removed the organ without any complication. Code the appendectomy procedure.

    _____

2. Blepharoplasty is necessary to correct visual obstruction issues on an otherwise healthy 82-year-old male who suffers from excessive skin weighting down his eyelid. The surgery is performed on the right upper eyelid. How should this be coded?

    _____

3. Manipulative treatment to three spinal regions was performed by a chiropractor on a Medicare patient to relieve severe acute back pain. The patient achieved moderate pain relief once the treatment was over. How should this be coded to report the acute treatment?

    _____

Certification Questions

1. Use of the modifier -GA describes what type of service?

    a. Waiver of liability on file   c. Service expected to be denied
    b. Glucose monitor supply for diabetic   d. Live kidney donor

2. What type of service is modifier -57, Decision for surgery to be used on?

    a. Surgical code   c. E/M code

    b. Anesthesia code   d. Medicine code

3. What modifier assists in the reporting of a procedure performed on the left great toe?

    a. -T3   c. -TA

    b. -T7   d. -TG

4. What scenario best describes the use of modifier -58?

    a. Return trip to the OR due to a hemorrhage

    b. Repeat procedure by the same provider

    c. Recurrent hernia repair on a 53-year-old

    d. Removal of tissue expanders immediately followed by surgery to cover a defect

5. Which symbol implies modifier -51 should not be used?

    a. ▲   c. +

    b. ⊙   d. ⃠

6. Which code would allow for a modifier -63 appendage?

    a. 33610   c. 21930

    b. 99464   d. 54150

7. Severe weather required the ambulance to transport the patient from her burning apartment to the nearest hospital instead of the burn center 35 miles away. What modifier should be used?

    a. -AH   c. -RH

    b. -TP   d. -UE

8. The admitting physician performed a comprehensive history and physical on a severely injured Medicare patient and relayed to her son that she would not survive without immediate surgery. Consent was given and the patient was taken to surgery immediately. Code the service.

    a. 99221   c. 99255-57

    b. 99223-57, AI   d. 99222-AI

9. What modifier should be used to report surgical services on a patient necessitating two surgeons' skills working together to perform and complete a particular procedure?

    a. -80   c. -69

    b. -62   d. -66

10. What does the reporting of modifier -PA on the claim form indicate?

    a. Service by a physician assistant

    b. Physical status abnormality

    c. Surgical procedure performed on wrong body part

    d. Service by a practicing associate

Billing and Collections

14

In assigning codes for diagnoses and procedures and linking these codes accurately to indicate the medical necessity, accuracy and completeness are important in the billing, reimbursement, and collections for services rendered in any health care facility. Billing begins with the patient information form completed prior to the patient being seen by the provider. This information should not be left there, however. It should be checked each time the patient returns to the office so medical and financial records are current and accurate.

Since initial contact begins when the patient calls the office to inquire about a practice and make an appointment, everyone in a medical practice needs to understand the patient information necessary to prepare the patient's medical record, establish the patient's account, collect copayment and coinsurance amounts, and submit claims to third-party payors.

The patient information form can be designed to obtain patient information exclusive to a particular practice and/or specialty. Many forms now request the patient's cell phone number and e-mail address. Others may ask such questions as the name a patient prefers to be called, such as a nickname, or how the patient learned about the practice. Information may also include policies on financial arrangements and late charges.

Name: _____   **Date:** _____

EXERCISES

Coding Exercises

Match the diagnosis with the procedure to show a valid linkage for medical necessity.

Diagnosis		Procedure
_____	1. Migraine headache	A. Mammogram
_____	2. Substernal chest discomfort	B. Needle biopsy
_____	3. Nocturia	C. MRI of lumbar vertebrae
_____	4. Family history of prostate cancer	D. Injection of Demerol and Phenergen
_____	5. Epilepsy	E. Ultrasound of gallbladder
_____	6. Liver function due to statin use	F. Steroid injection
_____	7. Cholecystitis	G. Urinalysis
_____	8. Tuberculosis	H. Puncture aspiration
_____	9. R/O diabetes mellitus	I. PSA
_____	10. Pancreatic carcinoma	J. Chest X-ray
_____	11. Family hx. of breast cancer	K. Vitamin B12 injection
_____	12. Cystic lesion of breast	L. Hepatic function panel
_____	13. Pernicious anemia	M. GTT
_____	14. Herniated L4–L5	N. EKG
_____	15. Bursitis of shoulder	O. EEG

Certification Questions

1. An established patient is seen in the Digestive Clinic for a detailed consultation for possible GERD. What is the correct code for the test that would confirm this diagnosis?

   a. 91010

   b. 91020

   c. 91030

   d. 91034

2. A patient is referred to an orthopedic surgeon for evaluation of bursitis, for which she was treated in the past by this physician group. A detailed history and exam are performed. Complete X-rays of the right shoulder confirm the bursitis. An injection of cortisone is administered into the right shoulder bursa. What is the correct code for the injection?

   a. 96372

   b. 96374

   c. 20605

   d. 20610

3. A patient diagnosed with morbid obesity is seen for consultation in the surgeon's office for a gastric bypass procedure. He completes the patient registration form for a new patient and presents his Medicare card with Aetna as secondary supplemental insurance. The visit today is a detailed history and examination. What is the correct E/M code?

   a. 43846

   b. 99203

   c. 99243

   d. 99253

4. When a second opinion is mandated by a third-party payor, what CPT modifier would be added to the E/M code?

   a. -25

   b. -32

   c. -57

   d. -62

5. A patient is prepped for a routine colonoscopy as an outpatient at the ambulatory surgery center. After administration of the IV medications and insertion of the scope, the patient has a seizure, and the physician discontinues the procedure. What CPT modifier would be used to indicate this?

   a. -52

   b. -53

   c. -73

   d. -74

6. A patient previously diagnosed with sick sinus syndrome is brought to the Emergency Department after experiencing tachycardia. Which one of the following would not be a procedure related to this diagnosis and these symptoms?

   a. 33202

   b. 93000

   c. 93224

   d. 95812

7. A routine screening mammogram is performed on a 44-year-old female with a family history of breast cancer. A two-view film study of each breast is taken. What is the correct CPT code?

   a. 77055-50

   b. 77056

   c. 77057

   d. 77057-50

8. A 75-year-old patient is followed in the nursing home for residual hemiplegia of the dominant side after a cerebrovascular accident three years ago. What is the correct ICD-9-CM code to report to Medicare?

   a. 434.91

   b. 436

   c. 438.21

   d. V12.59

9. A 58-year-old male complaining of chest pain has an electrocardiogram done in the office. The EKG is abnormal, showing nonspecific ST segment changes in leads V–VII. Further outpatient testing will be scheduled to rule out any cardiac disorders or abnormalities. How would this be correctly coded for reimbursement?

   a. Cardiac disorder, etiology undetermined

   b. Chest pain with abnormal EKG

   c. Noncardiac chest pain

   d. Probable myocardial infarction

10. What is the purpose of providing an insurance carrier with ICD-9-CM and CPT codes correctly linked to the patient's care?

    a. To complete the advance beneficiary notice

    b. To document the patient has medical insurance

    c. To provide for coordination of benefits

    d. To show the medical necessity for services and procedures performed

Review Questions

1. Review the patient information form in the textbook. Answer the following questions.

   a. What is the purpose of requesting home, work, and/or cell phone numbers?

   _____

   b. Why are the name and contact information of an emergency contact important?

   _____

   c. What should be done in addition to requesting insurance information on the form?

   _____

   d. Why would you question a condition related to an accident?

   _____

   e. How does the referral information relate to submitting an insurance claim?

   _____

2. An eight-year-old patient is scheduled for a tonsillectomy to be performed in the ambulatory surgical center. Since the patient has no insurance coverage, the parents arrange a payment plan with the surgeon's office with payments to be made monthly for six months. What financial form is completed for this procedure?

   a. Advance beneficiary notice

   b. HIPAA confidentiality form

   c. Surgical consent form

   d. Truth-in-lending agreement

3. Place an "x" in the space provided to indicate information to include on a patient statement.

   _____   Patient's name and address

   _____   Patient's date of birth/age

   _____   Date of service/procedure

   _____   Description of service/procedure

   _____   Patient's next of kin

   _____   Patient's telephone number

   _____   Provider's name, address, telephone number

   _____   Patient's chief complaint for service/procedure

   _____   Patient's social security number

   _____   Charges, payments, adjustments

4. The purpose of the Fair Debt Collection Practices Act is to protect consumers against abusive practices by debt collectors. In the space provided, put "T" for each statement that is true and "F" for each statement that is false as it relates to this act.

   _____   One cannot threaten to notify an employer that a consumer has not paid bills.

   _____   Calls are to be made between 8 a.m. and 9 p.m.

_____   The time difference in a region does not matter when calling for debt collection purposes.

_____   Embarrassing a consumer by advertising or publishing debt information is acceptable.

_____   A special collection fee can be added to the amount that is owed.

5.   Place an "x" in the space provided to indicate the correct procedure for billing for a deceased patient.

_____   Address the statement to the deceased at his or her last known address.

_____   Address the statement to the estate of (patient's name) mailed to last known address.

_____   Accept assignment when billing a third-party payor.

_____   Send the statement as soon as the patient expires.

_____   Contact probate court to check the status of the estate/will.

Filing the Claim Form

15

Understanding the concept of health insurance and how to complete the claim form for submission to the insurance carrier is an important part of the billing process, whether it is electronic claim filing or a traditional CMS-1500 claim form. The initial contact at the reception desk of a medical practice or patient registration at other facilities is the first step in the process of obtaining correct demographic and insurance information. This will allow coders and billers to abstract chart notes in order to submit claims to a third-party payor. In addition, understanding the reason for rejection or denial of a submitted claim assists in the resubmission of the claim or in the appeals process to the third-party payor.

A clear understanding of this process leads to accurate claims with correct payment to the provider. The insurance specialist must also be familiar with the various third-party payors and their individual requirements for claim submission and reimbursement. This includes knowing the status of participating versus nonparticipating providers and the medical necessity for services rendered, both in the office or outpatient setting and the inpatient facility.

Name: _____   **Date:** _____

EXERCISES

Certification Questions

To answer the following questions, refer to the CMS-1500 form.

1. A primary care physician refers a patient for outpatient physical therapy following a fracture of the tibia and fibula. What blocks of the CMS-1500 are required to designate a referring physician when the claim is filed by the physical therapy provider?

   a. 15 and 16
   b. 17 and 17b

   c. 24D and E
   d. 32 and 33

2. A patient is admitted to the hospital by the primary care physician for pneumonia on April 5. The PCP sees the patient daily on April 6, 7, and 8, then discharges the patient on April 9. The following days in the hospital are billed at the same level of CPT. What will be entered in Block 24G of the CMS-1500?

   a. 2
   b. 3

   c. 4
   d. 5

3. A patient is seen in the office for an eye injury sustained at work when a piece of metal he was welding went into his right eye. What block of the CMS-1500 must be marked to indicate a work-related injury?

   a. 10a
   b. 10b

   c. 10c
   d. 10d

4. A physician makes monthly rounds at a nursing home that provides skilled nursing services to its residents. What is the POS code required in 24B of the CMS-1500?

   a. 13
   b. 31

   c. 32
   d. 33

5. A retired patient has Medicare that is primary and an Aetna supplemental policy with his former employer. What block of the CMS-1500 is required for Medicare to cross over the claim to Aetna?

   a. 1a
   b. 9a–d

   c. 10a–c
   d. 11a–c

6. What is missing from the following CMS-1500 form that would reject the claim?

1. MEDICARE MEDICAID TRICARE CHAMPVA GROUP FECA OTHER	1a. INSURED'S I.D. NUMBER (For Program in Item 1)
[X] (Medicare #) [ ] (Medicaid #) [ ] (Sponsor's SSN) [ ] (Member ID#) [ ] (SSN or ID) [ ] (SSN) [ ] (ID)	
2. PATIENT'S NAME (Last Name, First Name, Middle Initial) 3. PATIENT'S BIRTH DATE SEX	4. INSURED'S NAME (Last Name, First Name, Middle Initial)
Smith James B MM DD YY 01 05 M[ ] F[ ]	Same as patient

© Cengage Learning 2013

7. A patient has a blepharoplasty of both upper eyelids performed by a well-known plastic surgeon. What is the coding error on the following CMS-1500 form that would result in lower payment of the procedure?

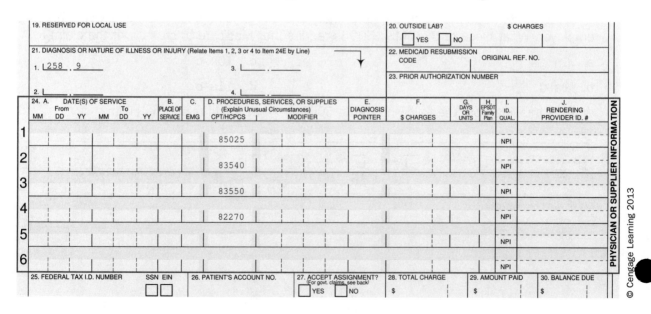

| 19. RESERVED FOR LOCAL USE | 20. OUTSIDE LAB? ☐ YES ☐ NO | $ CHARGES |
| 21. DIAGNOSIS OR NATURE OF ILLNESS OR INJURY (Relate Items 1, 2, 3 or 4 to Item 24E by Line) | 22. MEDICAID RESUBMISSION CODE | ORIGINAL REF. NO. |

1. 374 . 30   3.
2.   4.
23. PRIOR AUTHORIZATION NUMBER

24. A. DATE(S) OF SERVICE From MM DD YY To MM DD YY	B. PLACE OF SERVICE	C. EMG	D. PROCEDURES, SERVICES, OR SUPPLIES (Explain Unusual Circumstances) CPT/HCPCS | MODIFIER	E. DIAGNOSIS POINTER	F. $ CHARGES	G. DAYS OR UNITS	H. EPSDT Family Plan	I. ID. QUAL.	J. RENDERING PROVIDER ID. #
1			15822		850 | 00			NPI	
2								NPI	
3								NPI	
4								NPI	
5								NPI	
6								NPI	

| 25. FEDERAL TAX I.D. NUMBER ☐ SSN ☐ EIN | 26. PATIENT'S ACCOUNT NO. | 27. ACCEPT ASSIGNMENT? (For govt. claims, see back) ☐ YES ☐ NO | 28. TOTAL CHARGE $ | 29. AMOUNT PAID $ | 30. BALANCE DUE $ |

8. A patient is referred by Dr. Dogood to Dr. Bones, an orthopedic surgeon, for evaluation of pain in the left knee joint. An X-ray of the left knee reveals a torn medial meniscus. A CMS-1500 form is completed by Dr. Bones's office for the office visit and X-ray of the left knee, then sent to the insurance company. What is missing on the following CMS-1500 form?

17. NAME OF REFERRING PROVIDER OR OTHER SOURCE Robert Bones MD	17a.	18. HOSPITALIZATION DATES RELATED TO CURRENT SERVICES FROM MM DD YY TO MM DD YY
	17b. NPI	
19. RESERVED FOR LOCAL USE		20. OUTSIDE LAB? ☐ YES ☐ NO $ CHARGES

© Cengage Learning 2013

9. A patient diagnosed with anemia is sent to the lab for a CBC with differential, iron and iron binding capacity, and a stool for occult blood. What is the coding error submitted on the following CMS-1500 form?

| 19. RESERVED FOR LOCAL USE | 20. OUTSIDE LAB? ☐ YES ☐ NO | $ CHARGES |
| 21. DIAGNOSIS OR NATURE OF ILLNESS OR INJURY (Relate Items 1, 2, 3 or 4 to Item 24E by Line) | 22. MEDICAID RESUBMISSION CODE | ORIGINAL REF. NO. |

1. 258 . 9   3.
2.   4.
23. PRIOR AUTHORIZATION NUMBER

24. A. DATE(S) OF SERVICE From MM DD YY To MM DD YY	B. PLACE OF SERVICE	C. EMG	D. PROCEDURES, SERVICES, OR SUPPLIES (Explain Unusual Circumstances) CPT/HCPCS | MODIFIER	E. DIAGNOSIS POINTER	F. $ CHARGES	G. DAYS OR UNITS	H. EPSDT Family Plan	I. ID. QUAL.	J. RENDERING PROVIDER ID. #
1			85025					NPI	
2			83540					NPI	
3			83550					NPI	
4			82270					NPI	
5								NPI	
6								NPI	

| 25. FEDERAL TAX I.D. NUMBER ☐ SSN ☐ EIN | 26. PATIENT'S ACCOUNT NO. | 27. ACCEPT ASSIGNMENT? (For govt. claims, see back) ☐ YES ☐ NO | 28. TOTAL CHARGE $ | 29. AMOUNT PAID $ | 30. BALANCE DUE $ |

© Cengage Learning 2013

10. A patient is seen in the office complaining of rectal burning and discomfort, especially with bowel movements. Examination today reveals a perianal abscess. This is incised and drained and the patient will return in five days for recheck. What is the coding error on the following CMS-1500 form?

19. RESERVED FOR LOCAL USE		20. OUTSIDE LAB? ☐ YES ☐ NO	$ CHARGES

21. DIAGNOSIS OR NATURE OF ILLNESS OR INJURY (Relate Items 1, 2, 3 or 4 to Item 24E by Line)

1. L 682 . 2   3. L____ . ____

2. L____ . ____   4. L____ . ____

22. MEDICAID RESUBMISSION CODE | ORIGINAL REF. NO.

23. PRIOR AUTHORIZATION NUMBER

24. A. DATE(S) OF SERVICE From MM DD YY To MM DD YY	B. PLACE OF SERVICE	C. EMG	D. PROCEDURES, SERVICES, OR SUPPLIES (Explain Unusual Circumstances) CPT/HCPCS | MODIFIER	E. DIAGNOSIS POINTER	F. $ CHARGES	G. DAYS OR UNITS	H. EPSDT Family Plan	I. ID. QUAL.	J. RENDERING PROVIDER ID. #
1			46060					NPI	
2								NPI	
3								NPI	
4								NPI	
5								NPI	
6								NPI	

25. FEDERAL TAX I.D. NUMBER SSN EIN ☐☐	26. PATIENT'S ACCOUNT NO.	27. ACCEPT ASSIGNMENT? (For govt. claims, see back) ☐ YES ☐ NO	28. TOTAL CHARGE $	29. AMOUNT PAID $	30. BALANCE DUE $

PHYSICIAN OR SUPPLIER INFORMATION

© Cengage Learning 2013

Case Studies 1-7

In Case Studies 1 to 7, complete a CMS-1500 claim form for each patient's insurance plan as indicated in the patient information. Blank CMS-1500 forms can be found in the back of the workbook. CMS-1500 forms can also be downloaded at http://cms.gov.

Provider Billing Information

Physician:	Dalton Dogood, MD.
	Internal Medicine
Address:	2222 Oldenburg St
	Newtown, PA 12345
Phone:	(222) 777-1515
EIN:	65-2233456
NPI:	0123765891

Participates with Medicare, Medicaid, and most insurance plans

Hospital services performed at Getwell Community Hospital

8567 Tremor Rd

Newton, PA 12345

Hospital NPI 9096432102

Case 1

Patient Information		**Insurance Information**

Name:	Susie Jacuzzi	**Primary Insurance:** United Health Care
Address:	2551 Maker St., Apt. 1	**ID No.:** 4122907233
	Newtown, PA 12345	**Group No.:** 78900
Phone:	(222) 774-2987	**Policyholder:** Jack Jacuzzi
Date of Birth:	02/25/1995	**Policyholder DOB:** 11/04/1961
Occupation:	Student	**Employer:** GWC Corporation
Employer:	N/A	**Relationship to Insured:** Child
Gender:	Female	**Secondary Insurance:**
Marital Status:	Single	**Policyholder:**
		Policyholder DOB:
		ID No.:
		Group No.:
		Employer:
		Relationship to Patient:

Chart Notes

Patient: Susie Jacuzzi

Date: 06/15/20XX

This is a new patient seen in the office today for a rash of her lower extremities. She states she went hiking yesterday and noticed the rash with itching after she took a shower last night. She has used cortisone cream that she had at home to try to relieve the itching but her symptoms have continued. She is given an injection of Decadron-LA 1 mg IM right deltoid, and a prescription for Decadron-LA p.o.

If the rash does not clear with the medication, she will be referred to a dermatologist.

Diagnosis: Rash of unknown etiology

Dalton Dogood, M.D.

Account Information

Date	Procedure or Service	Charge
6/15/20XX	Office Visit, PF	$65.00
6/15/20XX	IM injection Decadron-LA 1 mg	$10.00
6/15/20XX	Decadron-LA 1 mg	$18.00

Case 2

Patient Information

Name:	Don Swan
Address:	106 Canal St.
	Newtown, PA 12345
Phone:	(222) 788-2322
Date of Birth:	03/03/1933
Occupation:	Retired firefighter
Employer:	Retired, Newtown FD
Gender:	Male
Marital Status:	Married

Insurance Information

Primary Insurance: Medicare

ID No.: 402229380A

Group No.:

Policyholder: Self

Policyholder DOB:

Employer:

Relationship to Insured: Self

Secondary Insurance: Mutual of Omaha

Policyholder: Self

Policyholder DOB:

ID No.: 402229380

Group No.: 610

Employer: Retired, Newtown FD

Relationship to Patient: Self

Chart Notes

Patient: Don Swan

Date: 01/10/20XX

Mr. Swan is seen in the office today for recheck of his blood pressure and antihypertensive medications. As noted last month, his B/P was 188/98. At that visit he was started on Norvasc 5 mg in an attempt to lower the blood pressure.

Vitals today: B/P is 142/82. Weight 196 1/2 lb. Pulse 76 and regular. Respirations 18.

His chest and lungs are clear. Heart rate NSR. He states he feels good and has had no problems with the medication. He will continue the Norvasc 5 mg one each morning. To return two months for recheck of his blood pressure.

Diagnosis: Benign hypertension

Dalton Dogood, M.D.

Account Information

Date	Procedure or Service	Charge
1/10/20XX	Office Visit, EPF	$58.00

Case 3

Patient Information		Insurance Information
Name:	Angela S. Smyth	**Primary Insurance:** Medicaid
Address:	2012 N. 5th St.	**ID No.:** 112612789003
	Weston, PA 12356	**Group No.:**
Phone:	None	**Policyholder:** Self
Date of Birth:	10/30/1975	**Policyholder DOB:**
Occupation:	Unemployed	**Employer:**
Employer:		**Relationship to Insured:**
Gender:	Female	**Secondary Insurance:**
Marital Status:	Divorced	**Policyholder:**
		Policyholder DOB:
		ID No.:
		Group No.:
		Employer:
		Relationship to Patient:

Chart Notes

Patient: Angela M. Smyth

Date: 07/01/20XX

This is a former patient returning to this office after living out of town the past five years. She has Type II diabetes. She also states she has been having frequent migraine headaches. She has been on Imitrex in the past for the migraines. She is in today for evaluation of her diabetes and her headaches.

Examination today: B/P is 118/68. Weight 165 lb. Chest and lungs are clear. Heart is normal. She states her blood sugar levels checked at home have been normal. HEENT normal.

Blood is drawn in the office today for a quantitative glucose to be sent to the lab. She is given a new prescription for the Imitrex 50 mg and Glucophage 500 mg. She will continue to check her glucose at home and report levels to this office. She will return for recheck in three months.

Diagnoses: 1. Diabetes mellitus, Type II

2. Migraine headaches

Dalton Dogood, M.D.

Account Information

Date	Procedure or Service	Charge
7/01/20XX	Office Visit, detailed	$65.00
7/01/20XX	Venipuncture	$10.00

Case 4

Patient Information

Name:	Thomas Thom	
Address:	678 Wildwood Ave.	
	Oldtown, PA 12359	
Phone:	(222) 642-2270	
Date of Birth:	08/11/1928	
Occupation:	Disabled	
Employer:		
Gender:	Male	
Marital Status:	Widowed	

Insurance Information

Primary Insurance: Medicare
ID No.: 212778989W1
Group No.:
Policyholder: Self
Policyholder DOB:
Employer:
Relationship to Insured:
Secondary Insurance: Medicaid
Policyholder: Self
Policyholder DOB:
ID No.: 10004304021
Group No.:
Employer:
Relationship to Patient:

Chart Notes

Patient: Thomas Thom

Date: 06/28/20XX

Patient called to state he was having difficulty breathing, especially when lying down. Just generally overall felt weak and shaky. He is admitted to the hospital as a direct admission.
Discharged from hospital 07/03/20XX to his home. He will be seen in my office in one week.
See hospital admission H & P and Discharge summary for treatment/meds.

Diagnoses: 1. Chronic obstructive asthma

2. Bronchial pneumonia

Dalton Dogood, M.D.

Account Information

Date	Procedure or Service	Charge
6/28/20XX	Hospital admission, detailed, low comp.	$175.00
6/29/20XX	Hospital care follow, EPF, mod. comp.	$85.00
6/30/20XX	Hospital care follow, EPF, mod. comp.	$85.00
7/1/20XX	Hospital care follow, EPF, mod. comp.	$85.00
7/2/20XX	Hospital care follow, PF, mod. comp.	$75.00
7/3/20XX	Discharge, 45 min.	$75.00

Case 5

Patient Information		Insurance Information
Name:	William J. Suey	**Primary Insurance:** BC/BS
Address:	2515 Best Rd.	**ID No.:** MR2500673109
	Weston, PA 12356	**Group No.:** 20553
Phone:	(222) 807-9331	**Policyholder:** Self
Date of Birth:	09/05/1954	**Policyholder DOB:**
Occupation:	Painter	**Employer:** Brothers' Painters
Employer:	Brothers' Painters	**Relationship to Insured:** Self
Gender:	Male	**Secondary Insurance:**
Marital Status:	Married	**Policyholder:** Self
		Policyholder DOB:
		ID No.:
		Group No.:
		Employer:
		Relationship to Patient:

Chart Notes

Patient: William J. Suey

Date: 02/02/20XX

He is a new patient in the practice seen today with a complaint of a "lump" in his left breast, nipple area. Examination today reveals a nodule in the areola of the left breast. There is some discomfort with palpation but no real pain. No other symptoms. The patient is scheduled for an ultrasound of the breast. The exam today includes a detailed history and examination with medical decision making of moderate complexity. He will return after the ultrasound.

Diagnoses: 1. Nodule in the areola of left breast, R/O carcinoma

2. Family history of breast cancer in mother and sister

Dalton Dogood, M.D.

Account Information

Date	Procedure or Service	Charge
2/2/20XX	Office visit, detailed/mod. comp.	$115.00

Case 6

Patient Information

Name:	Donna A. Dean
Address:	2103 Morris Way
	Oldtown, PA 12359
Phone:	(222) 642-8090
Date of Birth:	12/30/1980
Occupation:	Cashier
Employer:	Dolan's Dept. Store
Gender:	Female
Marital Status:	Married

Insurance Information

Primary Insurance: Cigna
ID No.: 333176694R10
Group No.: 30333
Policyholder: Donald B. Dean
Policyholder DOB: 07/14/1978
Employer: JAR Auto Mart
Relationship to Insured: Spouse
Secondary Insurance:
Policyholder:
Policyholder DOB:
ID No.:
Group No.:
Employer:
Relationship to Patient:

Chart Notes

Patient: Donna A. Dean

Date: 04/01/20XX

This established patient is seen today for routine yearly pelvic exam with Pap smear. She and her husband have decided they are ready to have another child and will discontinue present contraceptive measures. B/P today is 112/78. Weight 124 lb. She states she has no complaints today. No abnormalities are indicated in the course of this examination. Urinalysis done today in the office is normal. She will be called when the results of the Pap smear are received.

Diagnosis: Routine annual pelvic examination

Dalton Dogood, M.D.

Account Information

Date	Procedure or Service	Charge
4/1/20XX	Annual pelvic examination w/Pap smear	$135.00
4/1/20XX	Urinalysis, dipstick, nonautomated without microscope	$12.00

Case 7

Patient Information		**Insurance Information**

Patient Information		Insurance Information
Name:	Mayme B. Brown	**Primary Insurance:** Medicare
Address:	6711 Bumble Bee Ln.	**ID No.:** 301012245B
	Weston, PA 12356	**Group No.:**
Phone:	(222) 807-3340	**Policyholder:** Self
Date of Birth:	10/02/1929	**Policyholder DOB:**
Occupation:	Homemaker	**Employer:**
Employer:		**Relationship to Insured:**
Gender:	Female	**Secondary Insurance:** AARP
Marital Status:	Married	**Policyholder:** Aaron D. Brown
		Policyholder DOB: 05/09/1928
		ID No.: 33329057710
		Group No.: 2550
		Employer: Self-employed
		Relationship to Patient: Spouse

Chart Notes

Patient: Mayme Brown

Date: 02/25/20XX

This patient is referred to this office by Dr. Henry McHenry, with the complaint of her legs feeling "twitchy," with a burning sensation that keeps her awake most of the night. She usually has to get out of bed to walk when this occurs, which really does not relieve her symptoms. She states she has these symptoms at least four nights each week.

A detailed history and examination reveal she may have restless leg syndrome. It is explained to her this diagnosis is based on her symptoms; there is no X-ray or blood test to diagnose RLS. Her medical history reveals she is being treated by Dr. McHenry for hypothyroidism. It is explained to her that restless leg syndrome can be related to hypothyroidism, and she should continue the Synthroid prescribed by Dr. McHenry. The patient is given a prescription today for Neurontin as a trial for RLS. She will return here in one month for follow-up of her symptoms and the medication.

Diagnosis: Restless leg syndrome

Dalton Dogood, M.D.

Follow-up: 03/04/20XX

Patient returns today for follow-up. She has taken the Neurontin for one month and states her symptoms are much improved with the medication. She will remain on the Neurontin and be followed for this condition by Dr. McHenry, her PCP.

Dalton Dogood, M.D.

Account Information

Date	Procedure or Service	Charge
2/25/20XX	Office consultation, detailed	$210.00
3/4/20XX	Office visit, follow-up, PF	$65.00

Referred by Dr. Henry McHenry, NPI #2252607310

Case Studies 8-10

In Case Studies 8 to 10, complete a CMS-1500 claim form for each patient's insurance plan as indicated in the patient information. Blank CMS-1500 forms can be found in the back of the workbook. CMS-1500 forms can also be downloaded at http://cms.gov.

Provider Billing Information

Physician:	Kenneth Sharpknife, MD.
	General Surgery
Address:	8570 Tremor Rd.
	Newtown, PA 12345
Phone:	(222) 777-5600
EIN:	55-9099238
NPI:	2223678901

Participates with Medicare, Medicaid, and other insurance plans.

Hospital services performed at: Getwell Community Hospital

8567 Tremor Rd.

Newtown, PA 12345

Hospital NPI 9096432102

Case 8

Patient Information

Name:	Connie Y. Davidson
Address:	7318 Country Mile Ln.
	Newtown, PA 12345
Phone:	(222) 778-9241
Date of Birth:	01/31/1965
Occupation:	Administrative Assistant
Employer:	Wells Fargo Bank
Gender:	Female
Marital Status:	Married

Insurance Information

Primary Insurance: Metropolitan
ID No.: YMM501243389
Group No.: 5000
Policyholder: Self
Policyholder DOB:
Employer:
Relationship to Insured: Self
Secondary Insurance: BCBS
Policyholder: Brad R. Davidson
Policyholder DOB: 08/09/1961
ID No.: 333905022
Group No.: 20502
Employer: Driskell Pharmaceuticals
Relationship to Patient: Spouse

Chart Notes

Patient: Connie Davidson

Date: 07/25/20XX

Patient was brought into the Getwell Community Hospital Emergency Department with severe right-sided pain radiating to the LUQ. It began early this morning and has increased in severity throughout the day and into the night. She has nausea with vomiting and states she feels feverish with chills.
Examination reveals extreme pain and tenderness all over the abdomen, particularly in both right lower and upper quadrants. Temp. is 100.2. WBC is elevated at 18,000. CT scan of the abdomen reveals a ruptured appendix with generalized peritonitis.

In addition, she is hypertensive with a B/P in the ED of 208/104. She states she did not take her antihypertensive medication today due to being so ill.

She is taken to the OR for appendectomy performed by this surgeon. Her PCP, Dr. McHenry, is called in to treat the hypertension.

Impression: Ruptured appendix with generalized peritonitis

Kenneth Sharpknife, M.D.

Account Information

Date	Procedure or Service	Charge
7/25/20XX	Appendectomy	$1,200.00
8/16/20XX	Ins. Pymt. Rec'd	−$640.00

Case 9

For Case Study 9, file a claim for the balance remaining with the patient's secondary insurance policy.

Patient Information	**Insurance Information**

Name:	Tony Tigger
Address:	610 Tiger Rd.
	Oldtown, PA 12359
Phone:	(222) 595-1034
Date of Birth:	02/14/1998
Occupation:	Student
Employer:	
Gender:	Male
Marital Status:	Single

Primary Insurance: Medicaid
ID No.: 22160110103
Group No.:
Policyholder: Self
Policyholder DOB:
Employer:
Relationship to Insured:
Secondary Insurance:
Policyholder:
Policyholder DOB:
ID No.:
Group No.:
Employer:
Relationship to Patient:

Chart Notes

Patient: Tony Tigger

Date: 04/25/20XX

This patient is referred by Dr. Dogood for outpatient tonsillectomy and adenoidectomy. His mother states he has had chronic tonsillitis since age three. He was recently treated by Dr. Dogood for a severe sore throat. The tonsils continue to be enlarged and inflamed.

Preauthorization number for this outpatient procedure issued by Medicaid is 891026347.

Diagnosis: Recurrent chronic tonsillitis

Kenneth Sharpknife, M.D.

Account Information

Date	Procedure or Service	Charge
4/25/20XX	Tonsillectomy and adenoidectomy	$1,050.00
5/30/20XX	Medicaid Pymt. Rec'd	−$326.50

Refer to the previous account information. The procedure is an allowed service by Medicaid. What must be done with the balance remaining after the Medicaid payment is received in the office?

Case 10

Patient Information	Insurance Information
Name: William J. Suey	**Primary Insurance:** BC/BS
Address: 2515 Best Rd.	**ID No.:** MR2500673109
Weston, PA 12356	**Group No.:** 20553
Phone: (222) 807-9331	**Policyholder:** Self
Date of Birth: 09/05/1954	**Policyholder DOB:**
Occupation: Painter	**Employer:** Brothers' Painters
Employer: Brothers' Painters	**Relationship to Insured:** Self
Gender: Male	**Secondary Insurance:**
Marital Status: Married	**Policyholder:**
	ID No.:
	Group No.:
	Employer:
	Relationship to Patient:

Chart Notes

Patient: William J. Suey

Date: 02/20/20XX

Patient referred by Dr. Dogood following an ultrasound of the left breast that revealed a tumor in the areola. A biopsy revealed carcinoma of the areola of the breast. A radical mastectomy of the left breast was performed with admission for observation on February 20. He was seen in follow-up and discharged home the following day. He is to be seen in the office for recheck in five days. At that time discussion will be had as to referral for oncology evaluation and treatment.

Diagnosis: Carcinoma of the areola of the left breast
Kenneth Sharpknife, M.D.

Account Information

Date	Procedure or Service	Charge
2/20/20XX	Radical mastectomy, left breast	$1,125.00
2/20/20XX	Hospital admission for observation	
2/21/20XX	Hospital discharge, 20 minutes	

Review Questions

1. Which one of the following is not true of Medicaid?

   a. It is a medical assistance program for medically indigent low-income persons.

   b. It covers aged and disabled persons on SSI or QMB.

   c. It covers persons in institutional or long-term care facilities.

   d. It always serves as the primary carrier for medical coverage.

2. Which one of the following is not eligible for Medicare benefits?

   a. A 68-year-old male, retired, receiving Social Security benefits

   b. A 55-year-old male receiving Social Security Disability Insurance benefits for four years

   c. An 18-year-old pregnant female with gestational hypertension and diabetes

   d. A 72-year-old widow whose husband retired from the federal government

3. Which one of the following may be considered medically unnecessary by Medicare?

   a. Application of short-leg walking cast

   b. Experimental chemotherapy treatment for colon cancer

   c. Holter monitor to document and assess premature ventricular contractions

   d. Immunization for influenza and pneumonia

4. In which case would a Medicare claim be filed as secondary coverage?

   a. A 45-year-old disabled patient receiving SSDI benefits

   b. A 66-year-old patient working full-time

   c. A 72-year-old patient in a skilled nursing facility

   d. An 80-year-old patient receiving Medicaid benefits

5. What does the term "sponsor" mean for TRICARE/CHAMPVA patients?

   a. The insurance plan or program name

   b. The insured or subscriber, whether active duty, retired, or deceased

   c. The provider of the medical service or treatment

   d. The referring physician/facility

6. What is the largest single medical program in the United States offering benefits in all 50 states?

   a. Blue Cross Blue Shield

   b. Medicaid

   c. Medicare

   d. TRICARE

7. A patient is treated in the Emergency Department for a back injury after falling from a ladder in the storage facility in the plant where he works. He complained of dizziness prior to the fall, and his blood pressure today is elevated. His employer requests the worker's medical records from his primary care physician to determine if there is a history of hypertension or previous problems with blood pressure that may be related to the fall. A medical clerk faxes the requested information to the employer without the patient's authorization. What defines this breach of confidentiality?

   a. AFL–CIO

   b. CMS

   c. HIPAA

   d. Workers' compensation law

8. A patient is seen in the surgeon's office four weeks following an open cholecystectomy. The patient has done well with no complaints and is released to normal activities, including returning to work. How is the office visit coded?

   a. A follow-up office consultation

   b. A new patient office visit

   c. An established patient office visit

   d. As an element of the global surgical fee package

9. Which one of the following is *not* a nonphysician service?

   a. Audiologic testing

   b. Durable medical equipment

   c. Hospital admission through Emergency Department

   d. Parenteral and enteral nutrition

10. Which one of the following is the computerized database that providers use to check the eligibility of a TRICARE patient?

   a. DEERS

   b. HCFA

   c. MSDS

   d. RBRVS

Payment for Professional Health Care Services, Auditing, and Appeals

Previous chapters have provided instruction in the correct coding of services and procedures with appropriate linkage of the diagnosis, symptoms, or injury to establish the medical necessity. The importance of medical terminology has been demonstrated to correctly describe the patient's condition, injury, or problem, as well as accurately describe surgical procedures, diagnostic tests, and other medical services provided. The correct linkage of the diagnosis to the procedures validates the necessity of the physician's work and ensures that services are correctly reported to the insurance company. The result of this process leads to the reimbursement of these procedures and services.

Reimbursement is the action of being paid back or the receipt of remuneration in exchange for goods or services, such as for professional services rendered in the medical office. Reimbursement is received after a request for payment is sent in the form of a statement to the patient, or after an insurance claim, such as the CMS-1500, has been submitted. Upcoding, down coding, and unbundling codes must be avoided, and it is necessary to have an understanding of what constitutes fraudulent activity. Audits can reveal these activities, leading to possible refunds of overpayments and financial penalties.

It is important to understand when patients can be billed, as well as when they cannot be billed. Participation status with Medicare and contracts with other insurers determine what amounts can be billed to, and collected from, the patient, such as copayments, coinsurance, and deductibles. For example, a service may be billed for $92.00. The provider contract agreement may determine a payment of $18.00, with an adjustment or write-off of $74.00. The explanation of benefits or remittance summary or advice will address any amount owed to the provider, such as a copayment. In the example, there is no copayment required, as the adjustment amount was $74.00. The provider may not "balance bill" the patient.

When errors do occur, corrections must be made. This process may be as simple as resubmission of a claim, a telephone call to attempt to correct the problem, or a request for a formal appeal, which may be a formal letter or completion of a specific form.

Name: _____   **Date:** _____

EXERCISES

Coding Exercises

Select the appropriate answer from the choices given.

1. A five-year-old female is seen for a routine well-child exam required prior to attending kindergarten. She has been seen in this medical office since birth. She receives the required MMR vaccination. CPT codes submitted are 90707 and 90471. What code is missing, resulting in lower reimbursement of the charges submitted?

    a. 99211   c. 99241

    b. 99212   d. 99393

2. An established 52-year-old patient is seen in the office late for abdominal pain with projectile vomiting. The exam and history are documented as detailed with moderate-complexity decision making. The patient appears ill with the pain worse with palpation to the right lower quadrant of the abdomen. The physician makes arrangements for the patient to be admitted to the hospital directly from the office and dictates the visit as his H&P. The patient is seen again in the morning at the hospital. How is this coded?

    a. 99214   c. 99233

    b. 99221   d. 99253

3. A patient is seen in the office for severe headaches. There is a family history of carcinoma of the brain. An EEG is scheduled as well as an MRI of the brain to rule out a brain tumor. What are the correct ICD-9-CM codes to submit to the insurance company?

    a. 346.00, V16.7, 191.9   c. V10.85, 191.9

    b. 784.0, V16.8   d. 784.1, V16.8, 237.5

4. Dr. S. performs a total abdominal hysterectomy on a 45-year-old female referred by the hospital Emergency Department. Dr. T. assists Dr. S. in this procedure. What is the correct code to bill for Dr. T.?

    a. 58150   c. 58200-80

    b. 58150-80   d. 58263

5. A patient receives an allergy injection each week in the allergy clinic that has performed the testing and prepared the allergenic extracts. What is the correct code to bill to the patient's insurance company?

    a. 95115   c. 95144

    b. 95120   d. 95165

Review Questions

1. What is the definition of copayment?

   a. A specified dollar amount paid to the provider for each encounter per the patient's contract agreement with the insurance carrier

   b. A specified percentage paid for medical services after the deductible has been met

   c. An annual out-of-pocket payment for medical services before payment by a third-party payor

   d. Payment paid to an insurance carrier for insurance plan coverage

2. List five reasons a CMS-1500 claim may be rejected based on completion of the form.

   1. _____

   2. _____

   3. _____

   4. _____

   5. _____

3. Which one of the following is not true of the advance beneficiary notice (ABN)?

   a. It notifies the patient that Medicare may not pay for a service it may not consider medically necessary.

   b. The ABN is a written notice given to the patient after the service is rendered.

   c. CPT codes and the total financial obligation for payment must be listed.

   d. Sufficient information must be given as to the reason the claim may be denied.

4. When are new annual ICD-9-CM codes implemented for health insurance plans?

   a. January 1

   b. April 15

   c. October 1

   d. December 31

5. Explain how professional courtesy can be considered a fraudulent activity.

   _____

   _____

6. An employee in a clinical laboratory reports unbundling of laboratory health panels submitted to Medicaid, resulting in a lawsuit proclaiming this to be a fraudulent activity. What is the term for this lawsuit?

   a. Qui tam action

   b. Res ipsa loquitor

   c. Res judicata

   d. Respondent superior

7. What division of the DHHS is responsible for investigation and enforcement of fraud and abuse cases, as well as legislation?

   a. Health Care Financing Administration

   b. Occupational Health and Safety Administration

   c. Office of the Inspector General

   d. Office of Medicare Hearings and Appeals

8. A patient receives an explanation of benefits from his health insurance carrier with the following information:

Date of Service	Billed Charges	Copay Amt.	Payment to Provider
11/21/20XX	$95.00	$15.00	$38.56

What is the amount the provider must adjust per contract agreement? _____

9. A Medicare patient receives an explanation of benefits from her health insurance company, stating it is responsible for a charge denied due to medical necessity. What is the name of the notification form the patient was required to sign prior to the service being rendered in order for the physician to collect for the denied service?

  a. Advance Beneficiary Notice

  b. Notice of Medical Necessity

  c. Participating Provider Agreement

  d. Redetermination Request Form

10. A patient statement for a colonoscopy with EGD performed by an endoscopy group practice stated the following:

Date of Service	TOS	Charges	Adjustments	Insurance Payment
07/11/20XX	Colonoscopy	$1,408.00	$958.00	$375.00
07/11/20XX	EGD	$1,050.00	$1,050.00	$0.00

What is the amount billed to the patient? _____

11. What is meant by down coding?

  a. Assignment of a lesser/lower code than documentation warrants

  b. Reporting multiple codes instead of one specific code that describes the entire service

  c. Selection of a code higher than supported by the documentation

  d. Waiving of copayment, coinsurance, or deductible

12. Which one of the following is not the correct linkage of a procedure with a diagnosis?

  a. 99203, 81000, 599.0

  b. 84152, 600.00

  c. 90703, 90471, 034.0

  d. 92002, 367.4

13. Which one of the following contains an error in coding?

  a. ICD-9-CM code 574.60 with CPT 76801

  b. ICD-9-CM code 786.50 with CPT 93000

  c. ICD-9-CM codes 455.1 and 455.4 with CPT 46260

  d. ICD-9-CM code 724.2 with CPT 72132

14. A 26-year-old male is assigned the ICD-9-CM code 642.03 for the CPT code 80055. What is the error in this billing scenario?

  a. Age

  b. Code linkage

  c. Gender

  d. Invalid fifth digit

15. Six weeks later, Dr. S. sees a patient in the office for scheduled follow-up for posthysterectomy. She has done well with no complications and is released to resume normal activities. What is the proper procedure to bill this follow-up visit to her insurance carrier?

    a. It is billed as a new patient office visit.

    b. It is billed as an established patient office visit.

    c. It is included in the global surgical package.

    d. An ABN is signed by the patient as a noncovered service.

16. What blood test would be medically necessary for a patient with a coagulation disorder?

    a. Complete blood count

    b. Occult blood

    c. Potassium

    d. Pro time

17. A physician orders an electrolyte panel. What tests are included in this panel?

    a. CBC, TSH, CO2, potassium

    b. CBC, CO2, potassium, sodium

    c. CO2, chloride, sodium, potassium

    d. Calcium, glucose, potassium, sodium

18. Percutaneous allergy testing includes which of the following?

    a. Patch, prick, puncture

    b. Prick, puncture, scratch

    c. Mantoux, PPD, puncture

    d. Venipuncture, scratch, heel stick

19. In coding for anesthesia, what error is made in the following scenario that would impact reimbursement? A 59-year-old male receives general anesthesia for debridement of a second-degree burn, 5% total body surface. The patient has uncontrolled Type II diabetes. CPT code 01952-P1 is submitted to the insurance company for payment of this procedure.

    a. Incorrect anesthesia code

    b. Incorrect code for total body surface

    c. Incorrect physical status modifier

    d. Absence of a code for qualifying circumstances

20. What coding error is made in the following scenario that would impact reimbursement? A 62-year-old female is seen for a suspected nodule in the left breast. A mammogram and ultrasound confirm the nodule, and a biopsy indicates a diagnosis of carcinoma of the left breast. The patient has a simple complete mastectomy. The codes submitted to the insurance company for physician's billing for the mastectomy are 174.9 and 19180-RT.

    a. Incorrect linkage of ICD-9-CM and CPT codes

    b. Incorrect CPT modifier

    c. Incorrect ICD-9-CM code for gender

    d. Nonspecific ICD-9-CM code

Mock Certification Test

This is a mock or practice examination provided for preparation of the Certified Professional Coders (CPC) examination offered by the American Academy of Professional Coders (AAPC).

The CPC exam is a timed exam in which the examinee will have five hours and 40 minutes to complete the 150-question test. Students are encouraged to complete the following 150-question mock exam by using the alotted five-hour and 40-minute time specification to adequately prepare for the CPC exam.

117

Name: _____   **Date:** _____

1. A six-year-old girl is seen for chronic recurrent episodes of otitis media. A bilateral myrinotomy is performed for serous otitis media of both ears. Which codes are assigned for both the procedure and the diagnosis?

    a. 381.01, 69433

    b. 381.10, 69433-50

    c. 381.4, 69436-50

    d. 382.9, 69436-50

2. An established patient sees the urologist who has not been seen in over three years with complaints of hematuria and sudden onset of left abdominal pain. After a detailed history and examination with low-complexity medical decision making, the urologist sends the patient to radiology for an IVP. What are the codes for the urologist to submit to the insurance company?

    a. 99203, 599.70, 789.00

    b. 99203, 74400, 599.70, 789.00

    c. 99213, 74400, 599.70, 789.00

    d. 74400, 599.70, 789.00

3. Referring to Question 2, the IVP reveals a left ureteral calculus. The urologist schedules and performs a left extracorporeal shock wave lithotripsy with cystourethroscopy of a left indwelling ureteral stent. What are the correct codes for these procedures and diagnosis?

    a. 50590, 52330-51, 592.1

    b. 50590, 52332-51, 592.1

    c. 50590, 52332-51, 592.9

    d. 50590, 52332-51, 594.2

4. In coding the diagnosis "carcinoma of the liver metastatic to the pancreas," what does the term "metastatic" mean in this context?

    a. The liver is a secondary site.

    b. The pancreas is the primary site.

    c. The pancreas is a secondary site.

    d. It is unspecified.

5. A wound of the right thigh measures 2.5 inches in length. If 1 inch is equal to 2.54 cm, what is the correct CPT code for intermediate repair of the wound?

    a. 12002

    b. 12032

    c. 13121

    d. 13132

6. What is CPT's definition of Emergency Department?

    a. Hospital-based care available 24 hours per day, seven days per week

    b. Urgent care center available 6 p.m. to 8 a.m.

    c. Facility available nights, weekends, and holidays

    d. Any facility that provides emergency care at any time

7. What diagnosis would be linked to a barium swallow?

    a. Dysphagia

    b. Dysphasia

    c. Dysplasia

    d. Dysphonia

8. What codes are listed in Special Services and Reports of the Medicine section of CPT?

    a. Immunizations and injections

    b. Laboratory/pathology/radiology

    c. Preventive medicine

    d. Supplies, handling of specimens, medical testimony

9. A patient is seen in the office for evaluation of polyps of the nasal septum. What is the ICD-9-CM code?

    a. 471.0   c. 471.9

    b. 471.8   d. 478.29

10. Which one of the following is *not* a bone of the skull?

    a. Axis   c. Occipital

    b. Ethmoid   d. Sphenoid

11. A 35-year-old female was seen by her OB/GYN six weeks ago for her annual examination and discussion about contraceptive measures. She is in today for insertion of an IUD. What are the codes for this encounter?

    a. 11975, V25.11   c. 58300, V25.42

    b. 58300, V25.11   d. 58301, V25.11

12. What is the medical term for temporary closure of the eyelid by suture?

    a. Blepharoplasty   c. Tarsorrhaphy

    b. Canthoplasty   d. Tympanoplasty

13. An infant is seen in the pediatrician's office for her six-month well-baby checkup. She is a new patient to this office. She is given her third DTP vaccination. What are the codes for this visit?

    a. 99201, 90701, 90460   c. 99381, 90700, 90460

    b. 99381, 90701, 90471   d. 99391, 90701, 90460

14. A 65-year-old female is discharged from the hospital four days following an admission through the ED with nausea, chest pain, and difficulty swallowing. The diagnosis after ED evaluation and admission was initial acute myocardial infarction. The physician spends 30 minutes reviewing medications and activities with the patient and her family prior to the discharge. What are the codes for the discharge service?

    a. 99238, 410.90   c. 99217, 410.90

    b. 99238, 410.91   d. 99239, 410.91

15. What is the medical term for decreased level of oxygen in the blood?

    a. Hemoptysis   c. Hypoxemia

    b. Hyperopia   d. Hypoxia

16. A 71-year-old female is seen in follow-up in the physician's office for Type I diabetes mellitus and elevated blood pressure measurements. Her glucose level today is 550. Her blood pressure today is 220/120. She is admitted from this office directly to the hospital for uncontrolled Type I diabetes mellitus and malignant hypertension. What are the codes for this admission?

    a. 99221, 250.03, 401.0   c. 99221, 250.02, 401.9

    b. 99222, 250.00, 401.0   d. 99213, 99222, 250.03, 401.0

17. What structure separates the abdominal cavity from the thoracic cavity?

    a. Aorta   c. Intercostal muscles

    b. Diaphragm   d. Mediastinum

18. A patient wanting to increase his life insurance policy is required to have a history and physical examination for the insurance company. What are the codes for this encounter?

    a. 99401, V70.3

    b. 99450, V70.3

    c. 99450, V70.0

    d. 99456, V70.3

19. An established patient is seen in the ophthalmology clinic with the complaint of headaches and difficulty seeing objects close-up. An intermediate eye exam is performed with the diagnosis of presbyopia. Reading glasses were recommended. What are the codes for this visit?

    a. 92002, 367.1

    b. 92004, 367.4

    c. 92012, 367.4

    d. 92014, 368.2

20. A young man experiences blunt trauma to the head resulting in a subarachnoid hemorrhage. The patient undergoes an emergency craniotomy for evacuation of the hematoma of the brain in an attempt to save his life. Code the anesthesia for this procedure.

    a. 00210

    b. 00210-P4, 99140

    c. 00211-P5

    d. 00215-P5

21. Which one of the following blood cells is *not* a leukocyte?

    a. Erythrocyte

    b. Eosinophil

    c. Lymphocyte

    d. Monocyte

22. A patient is seen in the urgent care center for a subcutaneous cyst of the right forearm. An incision and drainage are performed without complication. What is the code for this procedure?

    a. 10060-RT

    b. 10080-RT

    c. 10160-RT

    d. 11400-RT

23. A patient sees the company physician with the complaint of something in his left eye. Examination reveals a foreign body embedded in the eyelid. The patient is referred to the ophthalmology clinic where the foreign object is removed without difficulty. What are the codes for the ophthalmologist to bill for this procedure?

    a. 65205, 930.0

    b. 67413, 930.9

    c. 67430, 930.1

    d. 67938, 930.1

24. Which one of the following is an example of a pathologic fracture?

    a. Colles fracture of the radius

    b. Depressed fracture of the skull

    c. Fracture of zygomatic arch as a result of automobile accident

    d. Hip fracture as a result of fall from a chair secondary to osteoporosis

25. A 72-year-old man is seen for urinary retention and an elevated prostate-specific antigen (PSA). He is referred to a urologist for further evaluation. What are the ICD-9-CM codes for this encounter?

    a. 600.91, 790.93

    b. 788.29, 790.93

    c. 788.20, 790.93

    d. 788.21, 790.93

26. A patient is treated in the ED for severe recurrent epistaxis after receiving a problem-focused history and exam. The posterior nasal area is cauterized and posterior nasal packs are applied to control the nasal hemorrhage. The patient is then sent home with instructions to see his primary care physician the next day to remove the packing and check the area. What are the codes to bill for ED visit and services?

    a. 30905, 99283, 459.0
    b. 30905, 99281-25, 784.7
    c. 30906, 99281, 784.7
    d. 30901, 99281-57, 784.8

27. A patient is diagnosed with basal cell carcinoma of the right auricle, helical rim. What is the site of this carcinoma?

    a. Cornea of the eye
    b. Flap of the ear
    c. Labia majora
    d. Upper chamber of the heart

28. A 21-year-old male is sent to the lab for a three-hour glucose tolerance test (GTT). He had complained to his primary care physician of tiredness and increased thirst. He does have a family history of Type I diabetes. What are the codes for this encounter?

    a. 82946, 780.79, 783.5, V18.0
    b. 82951, 780.79, 783.5, V18.0
    c. 82951, 780.79, 783.5, 250.00
    d. 82977, 780.79, 783.5, 250.00

29. A patient has a complete ultrasound of the abdomen, which proves acute cholecystitis with cholelithiasis. What are the codes for this procedure?

    a. 76700, 574.00
    b. 76770, 574.70
    c. 76700, 574.90
    d. 76705, 575.10

30. A 16-year-old patient is treated in the ED for whiplash injury of the neck and low back pain following an automobile accident. He was a passenger in the car. What ICD-9-CM codes are assigned for this incident?

    a. 847.0, 724.2, E819.1
    b. 847.0, 724.2, E819.9
    c. 959.09, 724.2, E819.1
    d. 959.09, 959.19, E189.1

31. What are the codes for anoxic brain damage secondary to accidental overdose of Nembutal nine months ago?

    a. 348.1, 909.0, E929.2
    b. 348.1, 909.0, E929.9
    c. 348.1, 909.5, E929.2
    d. 348.9, 909.0, E929.2

32. A patient with a recurrence of colitis has a colonoscopy performed. There is no evidence of polyps, tumors, or masses, but there is mild nonspecific edema and inflammation of the rectal mucosa. Biopsies are taken of this area. How is this coded?

    a. 45378, 45100, 558.9
    b. 45380, 558.9
    c. 45380, 569.49
    d. 45381, 558.4

33. An 18-year-old new patient is in the office with the complaint of vaginal discharge and itching. There is no odor. Pelvic exam is normal. A wet prep mount was performed, which is negative for *Trichomonas*. The diagnosis today is nonspecific vaginitis. What are the codes for this visit?

    a. 99201, 87210, 616.10
    b. 99202, 87210, 131.00
    c. 99211, 87210, 131.00
    d. 99212, 87210, 616.10

34. A 10-year-old boy, who is a patient in this office, is seen for severe poison ivy after attending Boy Scout camp one week ago. He has eruptions over both hands and arms and complains of itching. He is given Dexamethasone sodium phosphate 2 mg IM and a prescription to get Decadron to take orally for one week for the poison ivy. How is this coded?

    a. 99202, 96372, J1100 x 2

    b. 99201, 96372, J7638

    c. 99212, 96374, J1100

    d. 99212, 96372, J1100 x 2

35. A 33-year-old patient undergoes a hysteroscopy with biopsy and D&C for irregular menstrual bleeding. What are the codes for this procedure?

    a. 58120, 626.6

    b. 58555, 626.9

    c. 58558, 626.4

    d. 58579, 626.9

36. A 21-year-old runner developed pain in the distal right fibula. An X-ray of the tibia and fibula reveals a proximal displaced fracture of the right fibula. What are the ICD-9-CM and CPT codes?

    a. 823.01, 73590-RT

    b. 823.02, 73592-RT

    c. 823.10, 73580-RT

    d. 823.82, 73590-RT

37. A 19-year-old patient is seen in the clinic as a new patient for a problem-focused visit. She has not had a menstrual period for the past two months and suspects she is pregnant. A urine sample is obtained for a pregnancy test. She will be called by this office later today with those results. What are the CPT codes for this visit?

    a. 99202, 81000

    b. 99211, 81025

    c. 99201, 81025

    d. 99201, 99000

38. A patient has a rhinoplasty performed for a congenital deviated nasal septum deformity. The patient's health is good. What are the codes for the procedure and diagnosis?

    a. 30400, 738.0

    b. 30420, 748.1

    c. 30462, 745.0

    d. 30462, 754.0

39. Referring to Question 38, what is the anesthesia code for this procedure?

    a. 00160-P1

    b. 00162-P1

    c. 00170-P1

    d. 00190-P1

40. A toddler is brought into the urgent care center by his mother, who states the child has a marble stuck in his nose. The marble is removed from the nasal area without difficulty. What are the codes for this problem?

    a. 930.8, 30300

    b. 931, 30310

    c. 932, 30300

    d. 932, 30310

41. What is the medical term for mumps?

    a. Epidemic parotitis

    b. Rubella

    c. Shigellosis

    d. Varicella

42. A 17-year-old female is seen in the office after fainting at school. She states she had not eaten anything all day. It is noted she has had significant weight loss over the past three months. Her weight today is 107 lbs, down from 118 lbs last visit. Her mother states her daughter does not eat meals with the family and generally simply snacks at home. The impression for the visit today is anorexia nervosa. What is the ICD-9-CM code for today's visit?

    a. 300.11   c. 783.0

    b. 307.1   d. 783.21

43. A 63-year-old male with Type I diabetes mellitus, uncontrolled, is admitted to the hospital for regulation of his long-term insulin dosage. The patient had been in the hospital four weeks earlier for an acute myocardial infarction of the anterior wall. This will be rechecked during this admission. What are the ICD-9-CM codes for this hospitalization?

    a. 250.00, 410.02   c. 250.03, 410.10

    b. 250.02, 410.10, V58.67   d. 250.03, 410.12, V58.67

44. Fine needle aspiration with imaging guidance is performed for biopsy of the breast. How is this coded?

    a. 10022   c. 19102

    b. 19000   d. 19103

45. A patient comes to the physician's office with severe chest pain, shortness of breath, and marked perspiration. After examination and EKG, it is determined that he is having an acute myocardial infarction. 911 is called and the patient is taken to the hospital for admission to the coronary care unit. The physician who provided the emergency office services will be the admitting physician. Which category is used to code these services?

    a. Critical care services   c. Hospital inpatient admission

    b. Emergency Department services   d. Office or other outpatient services

46. What does the term occult mean when used to refer to testing a fecal sample for occult blood?

    a. Bright red blood   c. Parasitic blood

    b. Hidden or obscured blood   d. Tarry black blood

47. A 47-year-old patient is prescribed Lipitor for hypercholesterolemia. A lipid panel and hepatic panel are ordered to check cholesterol, triglycerides, and HDL levels and to check liver function due to the Lipitor. What are the codes assigned for the lab studies?

    a. 80050, 80061   c. 80061, 80074

    b. 80053, 80061   d. 80061, 80076

48. What body system contains the thyroid, parathyroid, and adrenal glands and pancreas?

    a. Digestive   c. Mediastinum and diaphragm

    b. Endocrine   d. Urinary

49. A drug screen for a new employee reveals a positive result for opiates. What CPT code is assigned to confirm the use of narcotics?

    a. 80101   c. 80103

    b. 80102   d. 80299

50. A continuous positive airway pressure (CPAP) device is initiated and managed for a 52-year-old patient diagnosed with sleep apnea. An apnea monitor with recording feature is obtained for the patient. What are the codes for these services and diagnosis?

    a. 770.81, 94660, E0618   **c.** 780.57, 94662, E0619

    b. 780.57, 94660, E0601   **d.** 786.03, 94660, E0618

51. What are the three key components for E/M services?

    a. Decision making, counseling, coordination of care   **c.** Physical exam, decision making, time

                                         d. Physical exam, counseling, time

    b. History, physical exam, decision making

52. A 70-year-old female is brought into the Emergency Department after falling in a parking lot and hitting the crown of her head against the license plate of a car, sustaining a 2.5 cm laceration of her scalp. Her vital signs are stable, and she states she simply slipped and fell on pavement that was slick after a rainstorm. The site is cleaned and injected with 2 cc of 1% lidocaine. Three 5-0 Dermalon interrupted sutures are used to close the wound.

Impression: 2.5 cm scalp wound

Plan: Patient is to follow up in one week for removal of the sutures or sooner if she develops any problems.

How is the repair service coded?

    a. 99281, 12001-25, E888.0, E920.8, E849.8   **c.** 12001, E888.0, E920.8, E849.8

                                         d. 12011, E888.0, E920.8, E849.8

    b. 12031, E888.0, E920.8, E849.8

53. A patient diagnosed with Raynauds has what symptoms?

    a. Constriction of the arteries with cyanosis of the skin   **c.** Pus in the pleural cavity

                                         d. Erythema and numbness of the skin

    b. Presence of excessive amounts of protein in the urine

54. Code the following office progress note.

S: Patient returns for a follow-up check of diabetes mellitus with cataracts. He has had diabetes for 10 years. Cataracts were checked today and it is recommended that he see his ophthalmologist for evaluation in the near future to determine his need for surgery. He states his diet is good and he has been going to the gym to work out. He is not having any other problems with the diabetes.

O: ROS including HEENT, neck, heart, lungs, abdomen, and extremities is unchanged from previous exam. PFSH is negative. He continues to smoke and reports drinking an occasional beer.

BP is 155/90. Weight 209 lbs

A: Diabetes mellitus, Type II, under control with no symptoms present other than the cataracts. Six of his toenails were trimmed in the office today.

P: Continue regular checkups and monitoring of diabetes, which includes home checks of his blood sugar, and document the readings. He will return for reevaluation in three months. He is reminded to see his ophthalmologist in the meantime to follow up with the cataracts.

What are the codes for this encounter?

    a. 250.00, 366.41, 11719 x 6   **c.** 250.51, 99213, 11719

    b. 250.51, 99212-25, 11719 x 6   **d.** 250.51, 366.41, 99213-25, 11719

55. Code the following SOAP report for a new Medicare patient.

S: This 66-year-old male was referred to this office by his PCP for consultation and evaluation of jaundice and nausea with RUQ abdominal pain. He states his wife noticed the jaundice a week ago. The pain has worsened over the past several weeks and has become more persistent on a daily basis.

O: Patient does not smoke and states he drinks only on the weekends when out with friends. The only surgery he has had is an appendectomy when he was 19 years old. Both parents are living and well. ROS demonstrates no previous problems or complaints with HEENT, lungs, heart, extremities, and abdomen in the past. NKDA.

BP 128/84. T 98.7°F. HEENT reveals head to normocephalic. PERRLA. EOMI. Lungs clear to percussion and auscultation. Heart demonstrates normal sounds. Abdomen has no palpable masses, but there is tenderness and guarding in the RUQ. No clubbing, cyanosis, or edema of his extremities. A recent hepatitis panel revealed abnormal studies with the SGOT and SGPT significantly elevated, indicating positive hepatitis B.

A: Acute hepatitis B.

P: Patient will continue with his PCP for further follow-up of the hepatitis and to monitor progress and possible development of any complications, including liver disease. He is given no medication today.

a. 070.20, 99203

b. 070.30, 99204

c. 070.30, 99242

d. 070.59, 99242

56. A 19-year-old man driving a motorcycle was injured when he skidded on wet pavement and hit a guardrail. He was seen in the ED and admitted to the hospital with the following conditions: lacerated liver, lacerated kidney, head injury without concussion, and fracture of C2 of the vertebrae. What ICD-9-CM codes are assigned upon discharge from the hospital?

a. 864.01, 866.02, 850.5, 806.00, E819.9

b. 864.01, 866.00, 959.01, 806.00, E819.2

c. 864.05, 866.02, 959.01, 806.00, E819.2

d. 864.05, 866.02, 850.5, 806.00, E819.2

57. The HCPCS category codes that begin with the letter L describe which type of service?

a. Durable medical equipment and surgical supplies

b. Drugs administered via IV, IM or subcutaneous

c. Orthotic and prosthetic supplies

d. Visual and hearing supplies

58. Code for the surgeon for the following operative note.

Preoperative Diagnosis: Cholecystitis; cholelithiasis

Postoperative Diagnosis: Cholecystitis; cholelithiasis

Procedure: Laparoscopic cholecystectomy

Anesthesia: General (administered by anesthesiologist)

Indications: This 24-year-old patient is seen in the ED for severe right upper quadrant abdominal pain radiating into the thoracic cavity. Ultrasound of the gallbladder indicates a diseased, nonfunctioning gallbladder with multiple stones. No stones are visualized in the common bile duct. Of note, the patient had a gastric bypass procedure almost a year ago.

Procedure: The patient was taken to surgery from the ED. She was placed in the supine position and general anesthesia administered. She was intubated, and a Foley catheter was inserted. She was prepped with Duraprep and draped in the usual manner. An upper midline incision was made for the previous gastric bypass procedure, and effort was made to place the incision laterally, but her abdominal wall was so lax that incision had to be made down through the anterior and posterior rectus. The peritoneal cavity was entered and Hasson trocar placed. She was positioned in reverse Trendelenburg and turned to the left. Under visualization, a 10.5 and two 5 mm ports were placed. The gallbladder was grasped and the cystic duct and artery were freed, clipped, and divided. The gallbladder was then dissected from the liver, grasped, and removed. No significant bleeding was noted. Trocar sites were infiltrated with 0.5% Marcaine and closed with 2-0 and 4-0 Vicryl. Steri-Strips were placed. She tolerated the procedure well.

a. 47562, 574.10

b. 47562, 574.10, V45.86

c. 47600, 574.10, V45.86

d. 47610, 574.12

59. Referring to the operative note in Question 58, what is coded for the charges for the anesthesiologist?

a. 00740-P2

b. 00790-P2

c. 00797-P2

d. 00840-P2

60. What does the term ABN stand for?

a. Abnormal

b. Advanced Beneficiary Notice

c. Auscultation, breath sounds, and noisey rales

d. Acute, benign neoplasm

61. A 15-year-old female is treated for a superficial sunburn to the forehead and cheeks from a tanning bed. What are the ICD-9-CM codes?

a. 692.71, E926.2

b. 692.82, E926.9

c. 692.82, E926.2

d. 941.07, E926.2

62. A group of nursing students observed a patient in CCU in cardiac arrest with a Code Blue called to the unit. All resuscitation efforts failed, and the patient was pronounced dead by the cardiac resuscitation team. The students were excited about this event in their training and discussed it at lunch in the hospital cafeteria with other students not assigned to their floor. What HIPAA rule was violated?

a. Abuse

b. Fraud

c. Breach of confidentiality

d. Breach of security

63. Code the following SOAP report.

S: Patient is seen today for follow-up of chronic angina and dyspnea. She states the angina still occurs mainly when she is resting, particularly when she first wakes up in the morning. This is accompanied by some dyspnea and pain occasionally radiating into the left jaw, but no palpitations. The angina is relieved by nitroglycerin tablets. She continues to take Inderal 40 mg q.i.d.

O: Vital signs today: BP–left arm–128/72. Weight 150 lbs. Chest is clear with no wheezing or rales. Heart has a Grade II/VI ejection murmur but no other abnormality heard today. A 12-lead EKG shows nonspecific ST-T-wave changes.

A: Unstable angina. Patient again refuses to consider cardiac catheterization.

P: New RX for Inderal 40 mg q.i.d. and refill on the nitroglycerin tablets. She will return for recheck in one month.

a. 99212, 93000, 413.9

c. 99214, 93005, 413.9

b. 99213, 93000, 411.1

d. 99214, 93000, 786.59

64. Code the following SOAP report.

S: Patient complains of generalized stiffness and general malaise. Her left knee has been swollen and felt "hot" for the past week. She was seen in this office 18 months ago for rheumatoid arthritis and was placed on Pencillamine and 2 mg prednisone b.i.d. Her other medications are loperamide for occasional loose stools and Tagamet 300 mg b.i.d. She denies shortness of breath or visual disturbance.

O: Examination reveals some swelling of the left knee with active synovitis and minimal fluid. Mild inflammation to hands and feet. Moderate stiffness in all four extremities, with restricted range of motion. No erythema. BP today is 116/72. Weight is 134 lbs. A complete automated CBC performed today is normal; automated sed rate is 65.

A: Active rheumatoid arthritis

P: The following recommendations are made:

1. Increase prednisone to 5 mg b.i.d. and Penicillamine to 500 mg b.i.d.

2. She is to have an X-ray of the left knee tomorrow and call for those results.

3. Recheck CBC and sed rate in four weeks.

4. Discussed with her the possibility of injecting steroids into the knee if she shows no improvement.

She is to return for recheck in four weeks. Code this service.

a. 99204, 85025, 85652, 714.0

c. 99214, 85025, 85652, 716.96

b. 99214, 85025, 85652, 714.0

d. 99214, 85004, 85651, 714.0

65. A 58-year-old female has her annual screening mammogram performed on July 5. A 2 cm mass is demonstrated in the left breast, so she returns for a diagnostic mammogram of the left breast on July 20. In addition, computer-aided detection with digital imaging is performed. What CPT code is submitted to the insurance company for the procedure performed on July 20?

a. 77055-LT, 77051-LT

c. 77057-LT

b. 77056-LT, 77051-50

d. 77057-LT, 77052

66. Referring to Question 65, the 2 cm mass is removed from the lower outer quadrant of the left breast. Pathology report indicates a fibroadenoma of the left breast. What is the final diagnosis code?

a. 611.72

c. 174.5

b. 217

d. 793.80

67. A patient is scheduled for a diagnostic colonoscopy in the ambulatory surgical center of a GI practice. He arrives at the center and Versed and Demerol are administered for moderate sedation prior to the procedure. Due to a fecal impaction causing blockage of the scope that cannot be removed with the use of enemas, the physician was only able to perform a sigmoidoscopy, inserting the scope to 18 cm. How would this be coded?

    a. 45330-52

    b. 45330-53

    c. 45378-74

    d. 45378-74, 45330

68. A new patient is seen in the office at the request of his PCP. He has recently moved to the United States from Iraq. An interpreter is called in to assist both the patient and physician with the language barrier. Due to this and the fact that the patient is somewhat agitated with the process, the office consultation takes 45 minutes longer regarding detailed counseling than what is considered the usual time for this comprehensive level 5 service. What is the CPT code for this encounter?

    a. 99205

    b. 99205-22

    c. 99245, 99354 x 1

    d. 99245-22

69. Code the following report.

    This 46-year-old male, well known to this practice, is seen today with complaints of fever, backache, and blood in the urine. He states the fever and backache began off and on about two weeks ago. He states the pain has gradually gotten worse in the last couple of days. ROS is negative for HEENT, lungs, heart, GU, GI, extremities, and neurological. He has been treated in the past for hypertension and takes Norvasc 10 mg to control it.

    On exam, the patient's BP is 142/86. Temp is elevated today at 100.2°F. HEENT: PERRLA. Head: Normocephalic. Throat is clear. No thyromegaly or adenopathy. Neck is supple. Heart: Normal S1 and S2 with no syncope, gallops, or murmurs. Lungs: Clear to percussion and auscultation. GU/GI: Patient does have guarding and tenderness in the lower abdomen. No palpable masses or tenderness. Extremities: Movement normal in all directions. Urinalysis including microscopic exam today is negative.

    Impression: Possible septicemia or urosepsis.

    Plan: Patient given Unasyn 1.5-gram. injection IM and a prescription for Cipro 500 mg p.o. b.i.d. He is to return to see me again if symptoms do not resolve in a few days.

    a. 038.9, 599.70, 99203, 96372, J0290, 81001

    b. 038.9, 599.70, 99213, 96372, J0290, 81001

    c. 780.60, 724.5, 99211, 96372, J0295, 81001

    d. 780.60, 724.5, 599.70, 99213, 96372, J0295, 81001

70. A patient undergoes an open reduction for a fractured humerus. What is the code for the surgical tray used for the procedure?

    a. 99070

    b. A4550

    c. A4625

    d. None, it is part of the surgical package.

71. What type of device would be implanted in a patient with cardiac conduction or rhythm disorders?

    a. Bougie

    b. Foley catheter

    c. Pacemaker

    d. Stent

72. A cardiologist performs an electrocardiogram on a 66-year-old male patient with a complaint of vague left chest pain radiating to the center of his chest. The first EKG is performed at 9:00 a.m. The patient is instructed to return for follow-up EKG at 1:00 p.m. and again at 5:00 p.m. The physician performs, interprets, and reports all three studies, which are billed accordingly by his office. What CPT codes would be assigned?

    a. 93000, 93000-76, 93000-59-76
    b. 93000, 93005, 93005-76
    c. 93000-76, 93000-76, 93000-76
    d. 93000, 93005, 93010

73. A patient is seen monthly in the office following pro times performed at the hospital laboratory to monitor long-term effects of the Coumadin that he takes for history of thrombosis. The nurse spends five minutes with the patient reviewing the results, checking the patient's vital signs, and confirming that the patient feels well. She notes change in the dosage is not necessary per physician orders. What are the codes for this encounter?

    a. 99078, 453.9
    b. 99090, 790.92
    c. 99211, V58.61
    d. 99212, 790.92

74. A patient is seen in the urgent care center after being stung by a bee. The patient has a history of allergy to bee stings. The patient's blood pressure during this encounter is elevated. The patient states he has hypertension and is treated by his PCP with prescribed medication. The hypertension would be coded for this encounter as a

    a. comorbidity or concurrent condition.
    b. complication of the bee sting.
    c. first-listed or primary diagnosis.
    d. principal diagnosis.

75. What is the purpose of the POS code required for CMS-1500 claim forms?

    a. To identify any modifiers required
    b. To identify if the patient is the policyholder, spouse, or other dependent
    c. To identify where the service was rendered/performed
    d. To list the number of days or units of the service or procedure

76. A 21-year-old new patient is seen in the urgent care center with the complaint of a nail perforating the palm of his right hand while working on an old piece of furniture. The physician took a brief history of the present illness, past and surgical history, and performed a skin inspection on both hands. The wound is treated by the physician and an injection of tetanus immune globulin, human, 200 mg is given in the deltoid muscle of the right arm. What CPT codes would be submitted for this encounter?

    a. 99201-25, 90389, 96372
    b. 99202-25, 90703, 90471
    c. 99211, 90389, 96372
    d. 99281-25, 90703, 96372

77. A five-year-old new patient is seen in the ER for a dog bite to his left forearm, measuring 3.5 cm. A problem-focused history and exam were performed by the ER provider. The wound is cleaned and a simple repair of the laceration is performed with the use of a sterile tray. He is given an injection of Ampicillin sodium 250 mg IM in the right gluteus medius. He does not need a tetanus shot. It is noted the dog belonged to a neighbor and has a record of rabies vaccinations. What are the codes for this encounter?

    a. 99202-25, 12002, 90389, 96372, J0290, 96372, 99070, 881.00, E906.0
    b. 99282-25, 12013, 90389, 96372, J0290, 96372, 99070, 881.00, E906.0
    c. 99202, 12003, 90703, 90460, J0290, 96372, 99070, 884.0, E906.0
    d. 99281-25, 12002, J0290, 96372, 881.01, E906.0

78. Code the following office note.

This new patient is in today complaining of SOB, wheezing, and cough productive of clear-white sputum. He has a long history of hypertension. He states he has difficulty breathing with exertion and just generally feels bad. Patient denies fever or chest pain.

Vital Signs: BP 186.108 right arm; 192/102 left arm. Pulse 92, slightly irregular. Respirations 22. Weight 202-1/2 lbs. Temp 99.8°F.

Exam today reveals blood pressure to be quite elevated.He states he currently takes Norvasc 5 mg for blood pressure control but cannot remember if he has taken the medication the last couple of days. Lungs contain many crackling rales and rhonchi bilaterally. Wheezes are noted bilaterally. Normal symmetry and expansion. Heart has a normal sinus rhythm without murmurs or gallops. He does have 2+ pitting edema of both feet. Neck is supple without lymphadenopathy, no JVD.

Procedures today in the office: EKG shows normal sinus rhythm. Rate is normal. AP and lateral chest X-ray done here in the office show pleural effusion increased in the right lobe of the lung. Blood is drawn for a CBC and electrolyte panel and sent to Quest for testing.

Impression:

　1. Asthma with COPD

　2. Congestive heart failure

　3. Benign essential hypertension

Recommendations:

　1. Lasix 40 mg one each morning for edema.

　2. Increase Norvasc 5 mg to two each morning for better control of blood pressure.

　3. Proventil Inhaler 2 puffs q.i.d.

　4. Albuterol 2 mg p.o. b.i.d.

He is to return for recheck in one week, or call sooner if his condition worsens. He will be called as soon as the chest X-ray results are received.

a. 99202, 93000, 71020, 36415, 493.20, 428.0, 401.9

c. 99205, 93000, 71020, 36415, 496, 428.0, 401.0

b. 99203, 93000, 71020, 36415, 493.20, 428.0, 401.1

d. 99205, 93000, 71020, 36415, 493.90, 496, 401.1

79. What condition do the acronyms IDDM and NIDDM relate to?

a. Arthritis

c. Diabetes

b. Cardiovascular disease

d. Pregnancy

80. How many codes are required to code a single group of internal and external hemorrhoids that are removed during the same session?

a. One

c. Three

b. Two

d. Four

81. What does the term epistaxis mean?

a. Headache

c. Hives

b. Heartburn

d. Nosebleed

82. A patient is seen by the PCP for a skin lesion of the right cheek, which is documented as a neoplasm of uncertain behavior. The patient is referred to a dermatologist for evaluation of the lesion. What is the ICD-9-CM code for the PCP to submit to the insurance carrier?

    a. 172.3   c. 528.9

    b. 172.8   d. 238.2

83. What is an example of an intermediate joint?

    a. Elbow   c. Knee

    b. Hip   d. Shoulder

84. A patient is diagnosed with carcinoma in situ of the breast. There is a family history of lung cancer. What are the correct codes?

    a. 174.9, V10.3   c. 233.0, V16.1

    b. 174.9, V16.1   d. 233.0, V10.3

85. What is meant by a disease or condition that is congenital?

    a. It is contagious.   c. It is present or existing at birth.

    b. It develops soon after birth.   d. It is a secondary disease or condition.

86. Where are the codes located for services provided by an urgent or immediate care center?

    a. Appendix A of CPT   c. Office or other outpatient services of CPT

    b. Emergency room services of CPT   d. Volume 3 of ICD-9-CM

87. What is the medical service for a follow-up of a patient seen initially in the office for a consultation?

    a. Follow-up consultation   c. Established patient office visit

    b. Initial consultation   d. Referral consultation

88. Which one of the following is *not* an example of an E code?

    a. Drowning in a bathtub   c. Family history of alcoholism

    b. Falling off a horse   d. Overdose of Sudafed

89. What is the code for an electroencephalogram, monitored for 55 minutes?

    a. 95812   c. 95816

    b. 95813   d. 95819

90. A six-month-old infant has an initial inguinal herniorrhaphy. What is the code for the anesthesia services for this procedure?

    a. 00830   c. 00834

    b. 00832, 99100   d. 00834, 99100

91. What section of CPT contains the codes for therapeutic injection services?

    a. Anesthesia   c. Medicine

    b. Evaluation and Management   d. Radiology/Laboratory/Pathology

92. What anatomical section is affected by COPD?

    a. Extremities   c. Lungs

    b. Intestines   d. Stomach

93. What are the codes for a patient admitted for an initial acute MI of inferoposterior wall, CHF, and hypertension?

    a. 410.21, 428.0, 401.9

    b. 410.31, 428.0, 401.9

    c. 410.40, 428.0, 401.9

    d. 410.80, 428.0, 401.9

94. A patient is admitted at 11:00 a.m. by the surgeon for observation following a septoplasty procedure for recovery and is discharged at 3:00 p.m. He is seen in follow-up at the office one week later by the surgeon. What are the appropriate codes to submit for the surgeon's services?

    a. 30520

    b. 30520, 99212

    c. 30520, 99234, 99238

    d. 30520, 99234, 99238, 99212

95. Which one of the following is an example of a symptom?

    a. Back pain

    b. Fracture of left tibia

    c. Laceration of right index finger

    d. Rash on forehead

96. What code is assigned for a work-related examination/evaluation by a physician other than the treating physician for the patient?

    a. 99056

    b. 99273

    c. 99455

    d. 99456

97. A patient has a urine pregnancy test performed by the lab using a visual color comparison test. What code or codes are used?

    a. 81025

    b. 81025, 36415

    c. 81025, 99000

    d. 84702

98. Which one of the following is an X-ray of the urinary tract?

    a. CABG

    b. IPPB

    c. KUB

    d. TURP

99. A physician sends a patient to the lab with an order for an electrolyte panel and a glucose. What are the correct codes for the lab to bill?

    a. 80048

    b. 80051, 82947

    c. 80053

    d. 82374, 82435, 82947, 84132, 84295

100. A 26-year-old female who is four months pregnant has Type II diabetes. This is her first pregnancy. There are no complications and the pregnancy is normal. What codes should be used?

    a. 250.00, V22.0

    b. 250.02, V22.0

    c. 648.80, V22.0

    d. 250.00, V22.2

101. A patient is treated in the urgent care center for a laceration of the chin requiring simple repair of a 3 cm wound. The visit today is a problem-focused history and exam of straightforward medical decision making. The patient is visiting relatives locally and has not been treated in this facility prior to this incident. He is told to see his physician when he returns home. What are the correct codes to bill for this encounter?

    a. 99201, 12002

    b. 99201, 12013

    c. 99281, 12013

    d. 99288, 12013

102. What is the medical term for difficulty with swallowing?
    a. Dyspepsia
    c. Dysphasia
    b. Dyspnea
    d. Dysphonia

103. Which one of the following is related to the term ESRD?
    a. Raynaud's disease
    c. Respiratory distress
    b. Renal disease
    d. Retinal disorder

104. A patient's chart notes a history of penicillin allergy. What code is used?
    a. V14.0
    c. V14.3
    b. V14.1
    d. 995.2

105. A physician orders a total serum cholesterol, lipoprotein, high density cholesterol, and triglycerides. What codes are used?
    a. 82465, 83718, 84478
    c. 82465, 83716, 84478
    b. 82465, 83715, 84478
    d. 80061

106. What is the medical term for incision of the vulva, usually done during labor to avoid laceration of the perineum during delivery?
    a. Colporrhaphy
    c. Orchiotomy
    b. Episiotomy
    d. Orchiopexy

107. When a consultation is required for confirmation by a third-party payor, such as Medicare, what is the modifier to use to indicate this with the appropriate CPT code?
    a. -21
    c. -26
    b. -22
    d. -32

108. Which of the following are *not* bones in the hand?
    a. Carpals
    c. Phalanges
    b. Metacarpals
    d. Tarsals

109. An established patient is seen in the office for a detailed history and exam for uncontrolled IDDM. His glucose levels checked at home have been running between 350 and 475. The patient also has cataracts related to his diabetic condition. What are the codes for this encounter?
    a. 99203, 250.53, 366.41
    c. 99214, 250.00, 366.41
    b. 99214, 250.53, 366.41
    d. 99214, 366.41, 250.53

110. Which one of the following is an eponym?
    a. Acquired immune deficiency syndrome
    c. Huntington's chorea
    b. Arteriosclerotic cardiovascular disease
    d. Poliomyelitis

111. A patient becomes agitated in the office and is given Valium 10 mg IM. What is the correct code for the medication?
    a. J2860
    c. J3360 x 2
    b. J3360
    d. J3490 x 2

112. A patient returns to the office for recheck of recently diagnosed pernicious anemia. The exam today is problem focused, and the decision has been made to give an injection of B12 500 mg IM. What are the correct codes?

    a. 99202, 96374, J3420, 281.0
    b. 99212, 96372, J3420, 281.0
    c. 99212, 96372, J3420, 281.1
    d. 99212, 96372, J3420, 285.1

113. A new patient is seen for multiple skin tags on the back of the neck and upper back/shoulder area. The office visit was expanded problem focused with straightforward decision making. Ten skin tags were removed by scissoring with electrocauterization of the sites. What are the correct codes?

    a. 99202, 11200
    b. 99202-25, 11200
    c. 99202-25, 11200, 11201
    d. 99213, 11200

114. What is the medical term for hives?

    a. Pediculosis
    b. Tinea corporis
    c. Urticaria
    d. Verrucae

115. What does alopecia mean?

    a. Acne
    b. Ringworm
    c. Shingles
    d. Hair loss

116. A 19-year-old male is diagnosed with noise-induced hearing loss from exposure to continuous loud music from MP3. What code indicates this?

    a. 389.9
    b. 389.14
    c. 389.8
    d. 388.12

117. What is meant by the term "etiology undetermined" when a physician describes signs or symptoms?

    a. Cause is unknown
    b. Caused by disease
    c. Caused by treatment
    d. No medical reason

118. A patient is followed in the nursing home for aphasia and hemiplegia following a CVA two years ago. What codes are used?

    a. 434.91, 438.11, 438.20
    b. 438.11, 438.20
    c. 438.82, 438.20
    d. 438.9

119. A five-year-old child is seen in the office for routine well-child check. The family is new to this practice. She is also given MMR and oral polio vaccinations. What codes should be used?

    a. 99201, 90707, 90712, 90471, 90474
    b. 99383, 90707, 90712, 90473, 90474
    c. 99383, 90707, 90710, 90460, 90461
    d. 99393, 90707, 90712, 90471, 90474

120. A myringotomy is performed on a three-year-old child with acute otitis media. What codes are used?

    a. 382.9, 69420
    b. 382.9, 69421
    c. 382.9, 69620
    d. 382.00, 69420

121. A 17-year-old female is admitted for loss of appetite and continuous habitual use of laxatives. How is this coded?

    a. 783.0, 305.91
    b. 307.1, 305.90
    c. 307.1, 305.91
    d. 995.84

122. A patient is seen in the GYN clinic for insertion of an IUD for birth control measures. She was seen one month ago for gynecologic exam, Pap smear, and counseling for the procedure. How is this coded?

    a. 58300, V25.02
    b. 58300, V25.11
    c. 58300, V25.13
    d. 58300, V25.42

123. A new patient is seen in the office for a detailed history and exam with direct admission from the office to the hospital for herpes ophthalmicus zoster. The admission is documented as a comprehensive history and exam with medical decision making of moderate complexity. He is followed in the hospital for two days at an expanded problem-focused level. The fourth day, the physician spends 45 minutes in discharge services for the patient. Code the hospital stay.

    a. 99203, 99222, 99232 x 2, 99239
    b. 99203, 99229, 99217
    c. 99222, 99232 x 2, 99239
    d. 99203, 99235, 99239

124. What are Braxton-Hicks contractions?

    a. Abdominal cramps
    b. Bladder spasms
    c. False labor pains
    d. Miscarriage

125. A patient has a colonoscopy because of a family history of colon cancer. During the procedure, two small polyps are removed by snare technique. How is this coded?

    a. 45315, V16.0
    b. 45338, V16.0, 211.3
    c. 45378, V16.0
    d. 45385, V16.0, 211.3

126. How does Appendix C of CPT assist providers?

    a. Provides information necessary for performance measure services
    b. Provides the full summary of revisions, deletions, and additions of the current year's CPT codes
    c. Provides the full listing and appropriate use of CPT and some HCPCS Level II modifiers
    d. Provides examples from a clinical perspective of presenting problems for certain EM codes

127. What does the term RBRVS stand for?

    a. Relative-Based Related Value Study
    b. Resource-Based Relative Value Scale
    c. Regional-Based Relative Value-Fee Scale
    d. Relative-Bound Related Value Scale

128. According to CPT surgical guidelines, what is considered a part of a surgical procedure and not ordinarily listed separately unless the technique substantially alters the standard management of a problem? The exception to this would be special circumstances that are provided for by separate code numbers.

    a. General anesthesia
    b. Special report
    c. Destruction
    d. Special prosthetics

129. Code 0106T is for a QST or quantitative sensory test performed by using touch pressure stimuli to assess large-diameter sensation. Where is code 0106T located?

    a. HCPCS Level II
    b. Medicine section
    c. Category II
    d. Category III

130. The pediatrician counseled the worried mother regarding the safety of immunizations for her five-year-old, who is set to start kindergarten soon. He reviewed vaccine/immunization information with her from a pamphlet from the American Academy of Pediatrics and answered all her questions regarding the DtaP-IPV components. She decided to proceed, and her child received a single combined IM injection of the DtaP-IPV immunization. What codes are used?

    a. 90700, 90713, 90471, 90472
    b. 90696, 90460, 90461 x 3
    c. 90696, 90471
    d. 90700, 90713, 90460, 90461

131. A 61-year-old man presented with persistently decreased vision, photophobia, and irritation in his left eye for four weeks. On exam, there was evidence of a nonhealing corneal epithelial defect. No infection was present. The physician admitted the patient and sutured a single layer of amniotic membrane to heal the defect. How should this procedure be coded?

    a. 65778
    b. 65780
    c. 65782
    d. 65779

132. A secondary procedure was planned to remove implants that were placed to stretch the skin to cover a large defect. What modifier should be appended to the secondary procedure?

    a. -78
    b. -76
    c. -58
    d. -59

133. A cancer patient required cryopreservation, freezing, and storage of blood-derived stem cells for transplantation at a later date. How should this be coded?

    a. 38207
    b. 38205
    c. 38208
    d. 38242

134. Which code does not not imply a description to use for either a unilateral or bilateral procedure?

    a. 69210
    b. 58900
    c. 58565
    d. 58940

135. What does the statement "rule of nines" refer to?

    a. A rule for assigning the 99000 series of CPT codes
    b. The common method used to calculate the percentage of total body surface area burned
    c. Fifth-digit classification when coding diagnosis
    d. Compliance terminology for a nine-step plan

136. When can destruction services be reported separately?

    a. When the destruction procedure is not a part of a greater procedure such as a surgery
    b. When utilizing electrosurgery only as the method of destruction
    c. When using cautery as a form of destruction to control bleeding in the OR
    d. Destruction can never be reported separately.

137. A rider twisted her ankle, suffering a severe sprain while dismounting her horse. An X-ray was negative for a fracture, and the provider placed her in a short leg cast to provide some stability and protection while walking. How should this be coded?

a. 29425

b. 29540

c. None. The cast application is part of the office visit.

d. 29440

138. According to CPT guidelines, which modifier is never to be reported with immune globulin or vaccine services?

a. -58

b. -76

c. -51

d. -90

139. In the Neoplasm Table, what column lists neoplasms that cannot be identified as benign or malignant conclusively according to pathology?

a. Primary

b. Benign

c. Ca in situ

d. Uncertain behavior

140. A patient received 12 minutes of chemotherapy infusion for her newly diagnosed cancer. How should this be coded?

a. 96413

b. 96409

c. 96360

d. 96413-52

141. Acupuncture services with electrical stimulation were performed for 45 minutes on a 29-year-old recovering from residual shoulder pain. How should this service be reported?

a. 97810 x 3

b. 97810, 97813 x 2

c. 97813, 97814 x 2

d. 97813, 97814

142. The visiting NPP provided mechanical ventilation care to a patient who was homebound. How should this service be reported?

a. 99504

b. 99341

c. 94005

d. 94002

143. Which modifer would be used to report an ambulance transporting the patient from his or her home to the hospital?

a. -RR

b. -RH

c. -HR

d. -HH

144. Thyroid imaging was necessary for a 49-year-old male recently diagnosed with a thyroid nodule to determine further diagnostic workup and possible biopsy. What CPT code should be used to report this service?

a. 78000

b. 78007

c. 78006

d. 78010

145. Code for an established patient returning to her opthalmologist after four years for a routine eye exam and new contact lens prescription, which is necessary for both of her eyes.

a. 92002, 92015

b. 92012, 92015

c. 92004, 92310-50

d. 92002, 92310

146. An 18-year-old female received ESRD-related services provided in the month of September. A complete assessment is performed at the beginning of the month with a second visit by her physician within the same week. The patient required hospitalization and hemodialysis shortly thereafter and remained in the hospital for two weeks. After discharge, she was closely followed by her physician who saw and evaluated her three more times before the end of the month. How should this service be coded?

    a. 90957

    b. Evaluation and Management Service

    c. Nothing, hemodialysis can only be reported.

    d. 90969

147. A 43-year-old female requires a paracervical block prior to D&C. How should the block be reported?

    a. Cannot code it, as surgery guidelines state blocks are an inherent part of the surgical procedure when performed at the same time

    b. 64435

    c. 01991

    d. 64630

148. What are the recognized follow-up days for minor procedures according to RBRVS?

    a. 0 and 10 days

    b. 0, 7, 10, and 14 days

    c. 10 days

    d. 90 or less days

149. What is the name of the form physicians must use for reporting their professional services to the insurance company?

    a. ABN

    b. CMS-1500

    c. UB-04

    d. PSF-1500

150. What does the acronym OIG stand for?

    a. Organized Internal Governance

    b. Office of Investigational Government

    c. Office of Inspector General

    d. Office of Internal Governance

1500

HEALTH INSURANCE CLAIM FORM

APPROVED BY NATIONAL UNIFORM CLAIM COMMITTEE 08/05

☐☐ PICA | PICA ☐☐

1. MEDICARE ☐ (Medicare #)   MEDICAID ☐ (Medicaid #)   TRICARE CHAMPUS ☐ (Sponsor's SSN)   CHAMPVA ☐ (Member ID#)   GROUP HEALTH PLAN ☐ (SSN or ID)   FECA BLK LUNG ☐ (SSN)   OTHER ☐ (ID)

1a. INSURED'S I.D. NUMBER   (For Program in Item 1)

2. PATIENT'S NAME (Last Name, First Name, Middle Initial)

3. PATIENT'S BIRTH DATE   MM   DD   YY   SEX   M ☐   F ☐

4. INSURED'S NAME (Last Name, First Name, Middle Initial)

5. PATIENT'S ADDRESS (No., Street)

6. PATIENT RELATIONSHIP TO INSURED   Self ☐   Spouse ☐   Child ☐   Other ☐

7. INSURED'S ADDRESS (No., Street)

CITY   STATE

8. PATIENT STATUS   Single ☐   Married ☐   Other ☐

Employed ☐   Full-Time Student ☐   Part-Time Student ☐

CITY   STATE

ZIP CODE   TELEPHONE (Include Area Code)   (   )

ZIP CODE   TELEPHONE (Include Area Code)   (   )

9. OTHER INSURED'S NAME (Last Name, First Name, Middle Initial)

10. IS PATIENT'S CONDITION RELATED TO:

11. INSURED'S POLICY GROUP OR FECA NUMBER

a. OTHER INSURED'S POLICY OR GROUP NUMBER

a. EMPLOYMENT? (Current or Previous)   ☐ YES   ☐ NO

a. INSURED'S DATE OF BIRTH   MM   DD   YY   SEX   M ☐   F ☐

b. OTHER INSURED'S DATE OF BIRTH   MM   DD   YY   SEX   M ☐   F ☐

b. AUTO ACCIDENT?   ☐ YES   ☐ NO   PLACE (State)

b. EMPLOYER'S NAME OR SCHOOL NAME

c. EMPLOYER'S NAME OR SCHOOL NAME

c. OTHER ACCIDENT?   ☐ YES   ☐ NO

c. INSURANCE PLAN NAME OR PROGRAM NAME

d. INSURANCE PLAN NAME OR PROGRAM NAME

10d. RESERVED FOR LOCAL USE

d. IS THERE ANOTHER HEALTH BENEFIT PLAN?   ☐ YES   ☐ NO   *If yes,* return to and complete item 9 a-d.

READ BACK OF FORM BEFORE COMPLETING & SIGNING THIS FORM.
12. PATIENT'S OR AUTHORIZED PERSON'S SIGNATURE I authorize the release of any medical or other information necessary to process this claim. I also request payment of government benefits either to myself or to the party who accepts assignment below.

SIGNED _____   DATE _____

13. INSURED'S OR AUTHORIZED PERSON'S SIGNATURE I authorize payment of medical benefits to the undersigned physician or supplier for services described below.

SIGNED _____

14. DATE OF CURRENT: MM   DD   YY   ◄ ILLNESS (First symptom) OR INJURY (Accident) OR PREGNANCY(LMP)

15. IF PATIENT HAS HAD SAME OR SIMILAR ILLNESS. GIVE FIRST DATE   MM   DD   YY

16. DATES PATIENT UNABLE TO WORK IN CURRENT OCCUPATION   FROM   MM   DD   YY   TO   MM   DD   YY

17. NAME OF REFERRING PROVIDER OR OTHER SOURCE

17a. |
17b. NPI |

18. HOSPITALIZATION DATES RELATED TO CURRENT SERVICES   FROM   MM   DD   YY   TO   MM   DD   YY

19. RESERVED FOR LOCAL USE

20. OUTSIDE LAB?   ☐ YES   ☐ NO $ CHARGES

21. DIAGNOSIS OR NATURE OF ILLNESS OR INJURY (Relate Items 1, 2, 3 or 4 to Item 24E by Line)

1. L___ . ___   3. L___ . ___

2. L___ . ___   4. L___ . ___

22. MEDICAID RESUBMISSION CODE   ORIGINAL REF. NO.

23. PRIOR AUTHORIZATION NUMBER

24. A. DATE(S) OF SERVICE From MM DD YY To MM DD YY	B. PLACE OF SERVICE	C. EMG	D. PROCEDURES, SERVICES, OR SUPPLIES (Explain Unusual Circumstances) CPT/HCPCS | MODIFIER	E. DIAGNOSIS POINTER	F. $ CHARGES	G. DAYS OR UNITS	H. EPSDT Family Plan	I. ID. QUAL.	J. RENDERING PROVIDER ID. #
1									NPI
2									NPI
3									NPI
4									NPI
5									NPI
6									NPI

25. FEDERAL TAX I.D. NUMBER   ☐ SSN   ☐ EIN

26. PATIENT'S ACCOUNT NO.

27. ACCEPT ASSIGNMENT? (For govt. claims, see back)   ☐ YES   ☐ NO

28. TOTAL CHARGE $

29. AMOUNT PAID $

30. BALANCE DUE $

31. SIGNATURE OF PHYSICIAN OR SUPPLIER INCLUDING DEGREES OR CREDENTIALS (I certify that the statements on the reverse apply to this bill and are made a part thereof.)

SIGNED _____   DATE _____

32. SERVICE FACILITY LOCATION INFORMATION

a.   b.

33. BILLING PROVIDER INFO & PH # (   )

a.   b.

NUCC Instruction Manual available at: www.nucc.org   ***PLEASE PRINT OR TYPE***   APPROVED OMB-0938-0999 FORM CMS-1500 (08-05)

Courtesy of Centers for Medicare & Medicaid Services.

1500

HEALTH INSURANCE CLAIM FORM

APPROVED BY NATIONAL UNIFORM CLAIM COMMITTEE 08/05

☐☐☐ PICA

PICA ☐☐☐

| 1. MEDICARE ☐ (Medicare #) | MEDICAID ☐ (Medicaid #) | TRICARE CHAMPUS ☐ (Sponsor's SSN) | CHAMPVA ☐ (Member ID#) | GROUP HEALTH PLAN ☐ (SSN or ID) | FECA BLK LUNG ☐ (SSN) | OTHER ☐ (ID) | 1a. INSURED'S I.D. NUMBER | (For Program in Item 1) |

2. PATIENT'S NAME (Last Name, First Name, Middle Initial)

3. PATIENT'S BIRTH DATE MM DD YY   SEX   M ☐   F ☐

4. INSURED'S NAME (Last Name, First Name, Middle Initial)

5. PATIENT'S ADDRESS (No., Street)

6. PATIENT RELATIONSHIP TO INSURED   Self ☐   Spouse ☐   Child ☐   Other ☐

7. INSURED'S ADDRESS (No., Street)

CITY   STATE

8. PATIENT STATUS   Single ☐   Married ☐   Other ☐

CITY   STATE

ZIP CODE   TELEPHONE (Include Area Code) ( )

Employed ☐   Full-Time Student ☐   Part-Time Student ☐

ZIP CODE   TELEPHONE (Include Area Code) ( )

9. OTHER INSURED'S NAME (Last Name, First Name, Middle Initial)

10. IS PATIENT'S CONDITION RELATED TO:

11. INSURED'S POLICY GROUP OR FECA NUMBER

a. OTHER INSURED'S POLICY OR GROUP NUMBER

a. EMPLOYMENT? (Current or Previous) ☐ YES ☐ NO

a. INSURED'S DATE OF BIRTH MM DD YY   SEX   M ☐   F ☐

b. OTHER INSURED'S DATE OF BIRTH MM DD YY   SEX   M ☐   F ☐

b. AUTO ACCIDENT?   PLACE (State) ☐ YES ☐ NO

b. EMPLOYER'S NAME OR SCHOOL NAME

c. EMPLOYER'S NAME OR SCHOOL NAME

c. OTHER ACCIDENT? ☐ YES ☐ NO

c. INSURANCE PLAN NAME OR PROGRAM NAME

d. INSURANCE PLAN NAME OR PROGRAM NAME

10d. RESERVED FOR LOCAL USE

d. IS THERE ANOTHER HEALTH BENEFIT PLAN? ☐ YES ☐ NO   **If yes**, return to and complete item 9 a-d.

READ BACK OF FORM BEFORE COMPLETING & SIGNING THIS FORM.

12. PATIENT'S OR AUTHORIZED PERSON'S SIGNATURE I authorize the release of any medical or other information necessary to process this claim. I also request payment of government benefits either to myself or to the party who accepts assignment below.

SIGNED _____ DATE _____

13. INSURED'S OR AUTHORIZED PERSON'S SIGNATURE I authorize payment of medical benefits to the undersigned physician or supplier for services described below.

SIGNED _____

14. DATE OF CURRENT: MM DD YY   ◄ ILLNESS (First symptom) OR INJURY (Accident) OR PREGNANCY(LMP)

15. IF PATIENT HAS HAD SAME OR SIMILAR ILLNESS. GIVE FIRST DATE MM DD YY

16. DATES PATIENT UNABLE TO WORK IN CURRENT OCCUPATION MM DD YY FROM   TO   MM DD YY

17. NAME OF REFERRING PROVIDER OR OTHER SOURCE   17a.   17b. NPI

18. HOSPITALIZATION DATES RELATED TO CURRENT SERVICES MM DD YY FROM   TO   MM DD YY

19. RESERVED FOR LOCAL USE

20. OUTSIDE LAB? ☐ YES ☐ NO $ CHARGES

21. DIAGNOSIS OR NATURE OF ILLNESS OR INJURY (Relate Items 1, 2, 3 or 4 to Item 24E by Line)

1. |___.___   3. |___.___

2. |___.___   4. |___.___

22. MEDICAID RESUBMISSION CODE   ORIGINAL REF. NO.

23. PRIOR AUTHORIZATION NUMBER

24. A. DATE(S) OF SERVICE						B. PLACE OF SERVICE	C. EMG	D. PROCEDURES, SERVICES, OR SUPPLIES (Explain Unusual Circumstances)		E. DIAGNOSIS POINTER	F. $ CHARGES	G. DAYS OR UNITS	H. EPSDT Family Plan	I. ID. QUAL.	J. RENDERING PROVIDER ID. #
MM	DD	YY	MM	DD	YY			CPT/HCPCS	MODIFIER						
1														NPI	
2														NPI	
3														NPI	
4														NPI	
5														NPI	
6														NPI	

25. FEDERAL TAX I.D. NUMBER   SSN ☐ EIN ☐

26. PATIENT'S ACCOUNT NO.

27. ACCEPT ASSIGNMENT? (For govt. claims, see back) ☐ YES ☐ NO

28. TOTAL CHARGE $

29. AMOUNT PAID $

30. BALANCE DUE $

31. SIGNATURE OF PHYSICIAN OR SUPPLIER INCLUDING DEGREES OR CREDENTIALS (I certify that the statements on the reverse apply to this bill and are made a part thereof.)

SIGNED _____ DATE _____

32. SERVICE FACILITY LOCATION INFORMATION

a.   b.

33. BILLING PROVIDER INFO & PH # ( )

a.   b.

NUCC Instruction Manual available at: www.nucc.org   **PLEASE PRINT OR TYPE**   APPROVED OMB-0938-0999 FORM CMS-1500 (08-05)

Courtesy of Centers for Medicare & Medicaid Services.

1500

HEALTH INSURANCE CLAIM FORM

APPROVED BY NATIONAL UNIFORM CLAIM COMMITTEE 08/05

☐☐☐ PICA   PICA ☐☐☐

| 1. MEDICARE   MEDICAID   TRICARE   CHAMPVA   GROUP   FECA   OTHER | 1a. INSURED'S I.D. NUMBER (For Program in Item 1) |

1. MEDICARE ☐ (Medicare #) MEDICAID ☐ (Medicaid #) TRICARE CHAMPUS ☐ (Sponsor's SSN) CHAMPVA ☐ (Member ID#) GROUP HEALTH PLAN ☐ (SSN or ID) FECA BLK LUNG ☐ (SSN) OTHER ☐ (ID)

1a. INSURED'S I.D. NUMBER (For Program in Item 1)

2. PATIENT'S NAME (Last Name, First Name, Middle Initial)

3. PATIENT'S BIRTH DATE MM | DD | YY   SEX M ☐ F ☐

4. INSURED'S NAME (Last Name, First Name, Middle Initial)

5. PATIENT'S ADDRESS (No., Street)

6. PATIENT RELATIONSHIP TO INSURED   Self ☐ Spouse ☐ Child ☐ Other ☐

7. INSURED'S ADDRESS (No., Street)

CITY   STATE

8. PATIENT STATUS   Single ☐ Married ☐ Other ☐   Employed ☐ Full-Time Student ☐ Part-Time Student ☐

CITY   STATE

ZIP CODE   TELEPHONE (Include Area Code) (   )

ZIP CODE   TELEPHONE (Include Area Code) (   )

9. OTHER INSURED'S NAME (Last Name, First Name, Middle Initial)

10. IS PATIENT'S CONDITION RELATED TO:

11. INSURED'S POLICY GROUP OR FECA NUMBER

a. OTHER INSURED'S POLICY OR GROUP NUMBER

a. EMPLOYMENT? (Current or Previous) ☐ YES ☐ NO

a. INSURED'S DATE OF BIRTH MM | DD | YY   SEX M ☐ F ☐

b. OTHER INSURED'S DATE OF BIRTH MM | DD | YY   SEX M ☐ F ☐

b. AUTO ACCIDENT? PLACE (State) ☐ YES ☐ NO

b. EMPLOYER'S NAME OR SCHOOL NAME

c. EMPLOYER'S NAME OR SCHOOL NAME

c. OTHER ACCIDENT? ☐ YES ☐ NO

c. INSURANCE PLAN NAME OR PROGRAM NAME

d. INSURANCE PLAN NAME OR PROGRAM NAME

10d. RESERVED FOR LOCAL USE

d. IS THERE ANOTHER HEALTH BENEFIT PLAN? ☐ YES ☐ NO *If yes*, return to and complete item 9 a-d.

READ BACK OF FORM BEFORE COMPLETING & SIGNING THIS FORM.

12. PATIENT'S OR AUTHORIZED PERSON'S SIGNATURE I authorize the release of any medical or other information necessary to process this claim. I also request payment of government benefits either to myself or to the party who accepts assignment below.

SIGNED _____ DATE _____

13. INSURED'S OR AUTHORIZED PERSON'S SIGNATURE I authorize payment of medical benefits to the undersigned physician or supplier for services described below.

SIGNED _____

14. DATE OF CURRENT: MM | DD | YY   ◄ ILLNESS (First symptom) OR INJURY (Accident) OR PREGNANCY(LMP)

15. IF PATIENT HAS HAD SAME OR SIMILAR ILLNESS. GIVE FIRST DATE MM | DD | YY

16. DATES PATIENT UNABLE TO WORK IN CURRENT OCCUPATION FROM MM | DD | YY TO MM | DD | YY

17. NAME OF REFERRING PROVIDER OR OTHER SOURCE

17a.
17b. NPI

18. HOSPITALIZATION DATES RELATED TO CURRENT SERVICES FROM MM | DD | YY TO MM | DD | YY

19. RESERVED FOR LOCAL USE

20. OUTSIDE LAB? ☐ YES ☐ NO $ CHARGES

21. DIAGNOSIS OR NATURE OF ILLNESS OR INJURY (Relate Items 1, 2, 3 or 4 to Item 24E by Line)

1. L___ . ___   3. L___ . ___

2. L___ . ___   4. L___ . ___

22. MEDICAID RESUBMISSION CODE   ORIGINAL REF. NO.

23. PRIOR AUTHORIZATION NUMBER

24. A. DATE(S) OF SERVICE						B. PLACE OF SERVICE	C. EMG	D. PROCEDURES, SERVICES, OR SUPPLIES (Explain Unusual Circumstances)		E. DIAGNOSIS POINTER	F. $ CHARGES	G. DAYS OR UNITS	H. EPSDT Family Plan	I. ID. QUAL.	J. RENDERING PROVIDER ID. #
From MM	DD	YY	To MM	DD	YY			CPT/HCPCS	MODIFIER						
1														NPI	
2														NPI	
3														NPI	
4														NPI	
5														NPI	
6														NPI	

25. FEDERAL TAX I.D. NUMBER   SSN ☐ EIN ☐

26. PATIENT'S ACCOUNT NO.

27. ACCEPT ASSIGNMENT? (For govt. claims, see back) ☐ YES ☐ NO

28. TOTAL CHARGE $

29. AMOUNT PAID $

30. BALANCE DUE $

31. SIGNATURE OF PHYSICIAN OR SUPPLIER INCLUDING DEGREES OR CREDENTIALS (I certify that the statements on the reverse apply to this bill and are made a part thereof.)

SIGNED _____ DATE _____

32. SERVICE FACILITY LOCATION INFORMATION

a.   b.

33. BILLING PROVIDER INFO & PH # (   )

a.   b.

NUCC Instruction Manual available at: www.nucc.org   **PLEASE PRINT OR TYPE**   APPROVED OMB-0938-0999 FORM CMS-1500 (08-05)

Courtesy of Centers for Medicare & Medicaid Services.

| | PICA | | | | | | | | | | PICA | |

CARRIER

1. MEDICARE	MEDICAID	TRICARE CHAMPUS	CHAMPVA	GROUP HEALTH PLAN	FECA BLK LUNG	OTHER	1a. INSURED'S I.D. NUMBER (For Program in Item 1)
(Medicare #)	(Medicaid #)	(Sponsor's SSN)	(Member ID#)	(SSN or ID)	(SSN)	(ID)	

2. PATIENT'S NAME (Last Name, First Name, Middle Initial)	3. PATIENT'S BIRTH DATE MM DD YY SEX M F	4. INSURED'S NAME (Last Name, First Name, Middle Initial)

5. PATIENT'S ADDRESS (No., Street)	6. PATIENT RELATIONSHIP TO INSURED Self Spouse Child Other	7. INSURED'S ADDRESS (No., Street)

CITY	STATE	8. PATIENT STATUS Single Married Other	CITY	STATE

ZIP CODE	TELEPHONE (Include Area Code) ( )	Employed Full-Time Student Part-Time Student	ZIP CODE	TELEPHONE (Include Area Code) ( )

9. OTHER INSURED'S NAME (Last Name, First Name, Middle Initial)	10. IS PATIENT'S CONDITION RELATED TO:	11. INSURED'S POLICY GROUP OR FECA NUMBER

a. OTHER INSURED'S POLICY OR GROUP NUMBER	a. EMPLOYMENT? (Current or Previous) YES NO	a. INSURED'S DATE OF BIRTH MM DD YY SEX M F

b. OTHER INSURED'S DATE OF BIRTH MM DD YY SEX M F	b. AUTO ACCIDENT? PLACE (State) YES NO	b. EMPLOYER'S NAME OR SCHOOL NAME

c. EMPLOYER'S NAME OR SCHOOL NAME	c. OTHER ACCIDENT? YES NO	c. INSURANCE PLAN NAME OR PROGRAM NAME

d. INSURANCE PLAN NAME OR PROGRAM NAME	10d. RESERVED FOR LOCAL USE	d. IS THERE ANOTHER HEALTH BENEFIT PLAN? YES NO If yes, return to and complete item 9 a-d.

READ BACK OF FORM BEFORE COMPLETING & SIGNING THIS FORM.

12. PATIENT'S OR AUTHORIZED PERSON'S SIGNATURE I authorize the release of any medical or other information necessary to process this claim. I also request payment of government benefits either to myself or to the party who accepts assignment below. SIGNED _____ DATE _____	13. INSURED'S OR AUTHORIZED PERSON'S SIGNATURE I authorize payment of medical benefits to the undersigned physician or supplier for services described below. SIGNED _____

PATIENT AND INSURED INFORMATION

14. DATE OF CURRENT: MM DD YY ILLNESS (First symptom) OR INJURY (Accident) OR PREGNANCY(LMP)	15. IF PATIENT HAS HAD SAME OR SIMILAR ILLNESS. GIVE FIRST DATE MM DD YY	16. DATES PATIENT UNABLE TO WORK IN CURRENT OCCUPATION MM DD YY MM DD YY FROM TO

17. NAME OF REFERRING PROVIDER OR OTHER SOURCE	17a. 17b. NPI	18. HOSPITALIZATION DATES RELATED TO CURRENT SERVICES MM DD YY MM DD YY FROM TO

19. RESERVED FOR LOCAL USE	20. OUTSIDE LAB? $ CHARGES YES NO

21. DIAGNOSIS OR NATURE OF ILLNESS OR INJURY (Relate Items 1, 2, 3 or 4 to Item 24E by Line) 1. ____ . ____ 3. ____ . ____ 2. ____ . ____ 4. ____ . ____	22. MEDICAID RESUBMISSION CODE ORIGINAL REF. NO. 23. PRIOR AUTHORIZATION NUMBER

24. A. DATE(S) OF SERVICE From MM DD YY To MM DD YY	B. PLACE OF SERVICE	C. EMG	D. PROCEDURES, SERVICES, OR SUPPLIES (Explain Unusual Circumstances) CPT/HCPCS MODIFIER	E. DIAGNOSIS POINTER	F. $ CHARGES	G. DAYS OR UNITS	H. EPSDT Family Plan	I. ID. QUAL.	J. RENDERING PROVIDER ID. #
1									NPI
2									NPI
3									NPI
4									NPI
5									NPI
6									NPI

25. FEDERAL TAX I.D. NUMBER SSN EIN	26. PATIENT'S ACCOUNT NO.	27. ACCEPT ASSIGNMENT? (For govt. claims, see back) YES NO	28. TOTAL CHARGE $	29. AMOUNT PAID $	30. BALANCE DUE $

31. SIGNATURE OF PHYSICIAN OR SUPPLIER INCLUDING DEGREES OR CREDENTIALS (I certify that the statements on the reverse apply to this bill and are made a part thereof.) SIGNED _____ DATE _____	32. SERVICE FACILITY LOCATION INFORMATION a. b.	33. BILLING PROVIDER INFO & PH # ( ) a. b.

PHYSICIAN OR SUPPLIER INFORMATION

NUCC Instruction Manual available at: www.nucc.org   **PLEASE PRINT OR TYPE**   APPROVED OMB-0938-0999 FORM CMS-1500 (08-05)

Courtesy of Centers for Medicare & Medicaid Services.

1500

HEALTH INSURANCE CLAIM FORM

APPROVED BY NATIONAL UNIFORM CLAIM COMMITTEE 08/05

☐☐☐ PICA   PICA ☐☐☐

1. MEDICARE	MEDICAID	TRICARE CHAMPUS	CHAMPVA	GROUP HEALTH PLAN	FECA BLK LUNG	OTHER	1a. INSURED'S I.D. NUMBER (For Program in Item 1)
☐ (Medicare #)	☐ (Medicaid #)	☐ (Sponsor's SSN)	☐ (Member ID#)	☐ (SSN or ID)	☐ (SSN)	☐ (ID)	

2. PATIENT'S NAME (Last Name, First Name, Middle Initial)

3. PATIENT'S BIRTH DATE MM | DD | YY   SEX   M ☐   F ☐

4. INSURED'S NAME (Last Name, First Name, Middle Initial)

5. PATIENT'S ADDRESS (No., Street)

6. PATIENT RELATIONSHIP TO INSURED   Self ☐ Spouse ☐ Child ☐ Other ☐

7. INSURED'S ADDRESS (No., Street)

CITY   STATE

8. PATIENT STATUS   Single ☐   Married ☐   Other ☐

CITY   STATE

ZIP CODE   TELEPHONE (Include Area Code) (   )

Employed ☐   Full-Time Student ☐   Part-Time Student ☐

ZIP CODE   TELEPHONE (Include Area Code) (   )

9. OTHER INSURED'S NAME (Last Name, First Name, Middle Initial)

10. IS PATIENT'S CONDITION RELATED TO:

11. INSURED'S POLICY GROUP OR FECA NUMBER

a. OTHER INSURED'S POLICY OR GROUP NUMBER

a. EMPLOYMENT? (Current or Previous)   ☐ YES   ☐ NO

a. INSURED'S DATE OF BIRTH MM | DD | YY   SEX   M ☐   F ☐

b. OTHER INSURED'S DATE OF BIRTH MM | DD | YY   SEX M ☐ F ☐

b. AUTO ACCIDENT?   PLACE (State)   ☐ YES   ☐ NO

b. EMPLOYER'S NAME OR SCHOOL NAME

c. EMPLOYER'S NAME OR SCHOOL NAME

c. OTHER ACCIDENT?   ☐ YES   ☐ NO

c. INSURANCE PLAN NAME OR PROGRAM NAME

d. INSURANCE PLAN NAME OR PROGRAM NAME

10d. RESERVED FOR LOCAL USE

d. IS THERE ANOTHER HEALTH BENEFIT PLAN?   ☐ YES   ☐ NO   If yes, return to and complete item 9 a-d.

READ BACK OF FORM BEFORE COMPLETING & SIGNING THIS FORM.
12. PATIENT'S OR AUTHORIZED PERSON'S SIGNATURE I authorize the release of any medical or other information necessary to process this claim. I also request payment of government benefits either to myself or to the party who accepts assignment below.

SIGNED _____   DATE _____

13. INSURED'S OR AUTHORIZED PERSON'S SIGNATURE I authorize payment of medical benefits to the undersigned physician or supplier for services described below.

SIGNED _____

14. DATE OF CURRENT: MM | DD | YY   ◀ ILLNESS (First symptom) OR INJURY (Accident) OR PREGNANCY(LMP)

15. IF PATIENT HAS HAD SAME OR SIMILAR ILLNESS. GIVE FIRST DATE MM | DD | YY

16. DATES PATIENT UNABLE TO WORK IN CURRENT OCCUPATION FROM MM | DD | YY TO MM | DD | YY

17. NAME OF REFERRING PROVIDER OR OTHER SOURCE

17a.
17b. NPI

18. HOSPITALIZATION DATES RELATED TO CURRENT SERVICES FROM MM | DD | YY TO MM | DD | YY

19. RESERVED FOR LOCAL USE

20. OUTSIDE LAB?   ☐ YES   ☐ NO $ CHARGES

21. DIAGNOSIS OR NATURE OF ILLNESS OR INJURY (Relate Items 1, 2, 3 or 4 to Item 24E by Line)

1. L___ . ___   3. L___ . ___

2. L___ . ___   4. L___ . ___

22. MEDICAID RESUBMISSION CODE   ORIGINAL REF. NO.

23. PRIOR AUTHORIZATION NUMBER

24. A. DATE(S) OF SERVICE						B. PLACE OF SERVICE	C. EMG	D. PROCEDURES, SERVICES, OR SUPPLIES (Explain Unusual Circumstances)		E. DIAGNOSIS POINTER	F. $ CHARGES	G. DAYS OR UNITS	H. EPSDT Family Plan	I. ID. QUAL.	J. RENDERING PROVIDER ID. #
From MM	DD	YY	To MM	DD	YY			CPT/HCPCS	MODIFIER						
1														NPI	
2														NPI	
3														NPI	
4														NPI	
5														NPI	
6														NPI	

25. FEDERAL TAX I.D. NUMBER   SSN ☐ EIN ☐

26. PATIENT'S ACCOUNT NO.

27. ACCEPT ASSIGNMENT? (For govt. claims, see back)   ☐ YES   ☐ NO

28. TOTAL CHARGE $

29. AMOUNT PAID $

30. BALANCE DUE $

31. SIGNATURE OF PHYSICIAN OR SUPPLIER INCLUDING DEGREES OR CREDENTIALS (I certify that the statements on the reverse apply to this bill and are made a part thereof.)

SIGNED _____   DATE _____

32. SERVICE FACILITY LOCATION INFORMATION

a.   b.

33. BILLING PROVIDER INFO & PH # (   )

a.   b.

NUCC Instruction Manual available at: www.nucc.org   **PLEASE PRINT OR TYPE**   APPROVED OMB-0938-0999 FORM CMS-1500 (08-05)

Courtesy of Centers for Medicare & Medicaid Services.

1500

HEALTH INSURANCE CLAIM FORM

APPROVED BY NATIONAL UNIFORM CLAIM COMMITTEE 08/05

☐☐☐ PICA | PICA ☐☐☐

1. MEDICARE ☐ (Medicare #) MEDICAID ☐ (Medicaid #) TRICARE CHAMPUS ☐ (Sponsor's SSN) CHAMPVA ☐ (Member ID#) GROUP HEALTH PLAN ☐ (SSN or ID) FECA BLK LUNG ☐ (SSN) OTHER ☐ (ID)

1a. INSURED'S I.D. NUMBER   (For Program in Item 1)

2. PATIENT'S NAME (Last Name, First Name, Middle Initial)

3. PATIENT'S BIRTH DATE   MM   DD   YY   SEX   M ☐   F ☐

4. INSURED'S NAME (Last Name, First Name, Middle Initial)

5. PATIENT'S ADDRESS (No., Street)

6. PATIENT RELATIONSHIP TO INSURED   Self ☐ Spouse ☐ Child ☐ Other ☐

7. INSURED'S ADDRESS (No., Street)

CITY | STATE

8. PATIENT STATUS   Single ☐ Married ☐ Other ☐   Employed ☐   Full-Time Student ☐   Part-Time Student ☐

CITY | STATE

ZIP CODE | TELEPHONE (Include Area Code) ( )

ZIP CODE | TELEPHONE (Include Area Code) ( )

9. OTHER INSURED'S NAME (Last Name, First Name, Middle Initial)

10. IS PATIENT'S CONDITION RELATED TO:

11. INSURED'S POLICY GROUP OR FECA NUMBER

a. OTHER INSURED'S POLICY OR GROUP NUMBER

a. EMPLOYMENT? (Current or Previous)   YES ☐   NO ☐

a. INSURED'S DATE OF BIRTH   MM   DD   YY   SEX   M ☐   F ☐

b. OTHER INSURED'S DATE OF BIRTH   MM   DD   YY   SEX   M ☐   F ☐

b. AUTO ACCIDENT?   PLACE (State)   YES ☐   NO ☐

b. EMPLOYER'S NAME OR SCHOOL NAME

c. EMPLOYER'S NAME OR SCHOOL NAME

c. OTHER ACCIDENT?   YES ☐   NO ☐

c. INSURANCE PLAN NAME OR PROGRAM NAME

d. INSURANCE PLAN NAME OR PROGRAM NAME

10d. RESERVED FOR LOCAL USE

d. IS THERE ANOTHER HEALTH BENEFIT PLAN?   YES ☐   NO ☐   If yes, return to and complete item 9 a-d.

READ BACK OF FORM BEFORE COMPLETING & SIGNING THIS FORM.
12. PATIENT'S OR AUTHORIZED PERSON'S SIGNATURE I authorize the release of any medical or other information necessary to process this claim. I also request payment of government benefits either to myself or to the party who accepts assignment below.

SIGNED _____   DATE _____

13. INSURED'S OR AUTHORIZED PERSON'S SIGNATURE I authorize payment of medical benefits to the undersigned physician or supplier for services described below.

SIGNED _____

14. DATE OF CURRENT: MM   DD   YY   ◄ ILLNESS (First symptom) OR INJURY (Accident) OR PREGNANCY(LMP)

15. IF PATIENT HAS HAD SAME OR SIMILAR ILLNESS. GIVE FIRST DATE   MM   DD   YY

16. DATES PATIENT UNABLE TO WORK IN CURRENT OCCUPATION   FROM   MM   DD   YY   TO   MM   DD   YY

17. NAME OF REFERRING PROVIDER OR OTHER SOURCE

17a.
17b. NPI

18. HOSPITALIZATION DATES RELATED TO CURRENT SERVICES   FROM   MM   DD   YY   TO   MM   DD   YY

19. RESERVED FOR LOCAL USE

20. OUTSIDE LAB?   YES ☐   NO ☐ $ CHARGES

21. DIAGNOSIS OR NATURE OF ILLNESS OR INJURY (Relate Items 1, 2, 3 or 4 to Item 24E by Line)

1. |___.___| 3. |___.___|

2. |___.___| 4. |___.___|

22. MEDICAID RESUBMISSION CODE   ORIGINAL REF. NO.

23. PRIOR AUTHORIZATION NUMBER

24. A. DATE(S) OF SERVICE					B. PLACE OF SERVICE	C. EMG	D. PROCEDURES, SERVICES, OR SUPPLIES (Explain Unusual Circumstances)		E. DIAGNOSIS POINTER	F. $ CHARGES	G. DAYS OR UNITS	H. EPSDT Family Plan	I. ID. QUAL.	J. RENDERING PROVIDER ID. #
From MM DD YY			To MM DD YY				CPT/HCPCS	MODIFIER						
1													NPI	
2													NPI	
3													NPI	
4													NPI	
5													NPI	
6													NPI	

25. FEDERAL TAX I.D. NUMBER   SSN ☐ EIN ☐

26. PATIENT'S ACCOUNT NO.

27. ACCEPT ASSIGNMENT? (For govt. claims, see back)   YES ☐   NO ☐

28. TOTAL CHARGE $

29. AMOUNT PAID $

30. BALANCE DUE $

31. SIGNATURE OF PHYSICIAN OR SUPPLIER INCLUDING DEGREES OR CREDENTIALS (I certify that the statements on the reverse apply to this bill and are made a part thereof.)

SIGNED _____   DATE _____

32. SERVICE FACILITY LOCATION INFORMATION

a. NPI   b.

33. BILLING PROVIDER INFO & PH # ( )

a. NPI   b.

NUCC Instruction Manual available at: www.nucc.org

PLEASE PRINT OR TYPE

APPROVED OMB-0938-0999 FORM CMS-1500 (08-05)

Courtesy of Centers for Medicare & Medicaid Services.

1500

HEALTH INSURANCE CLAIM FORM

APPROVED BY NATIONAL UNIFORM CLAIM COMMITTEE 08/05

| | | PICA | | | | | | | | | PICA | |

1. MEDICARE (Medicare #)   **MEDICAID** (Medicaid #)   **TRICARE CHAMPUS** (Sponsor's SSN)   **CHAMPVA** (Member ID#)   **GROUP HEALTH PLAN** (SSN or ID)   **FECA BLK LUNG** (SSN)   **OTHER** (ID)

1a. INSURED'S I.D. NUMBER (For Program in Item 1)

2. PATIENT'S NAME (Last Name, First Name, Middle Initial)

3. PATIENT'S BIRTH DATE MM | DD | YY   **SEX** M ☐ F ☐

4. INSURED'S NAME (Last Name, First Name, Middle Initial)

5. PATIENT'S ADDRESS (No., Street)

6. PATIENT RELATIONSHIP TO INSURED Self ☐ Spouse ☐ Child ☐ Other ☐

7. INSURED'S ADDRESS (No., Street)

CITY   **STATE**

8. PATIENT STATUS Single ☐ Married ☐ Other ☐   Employed ☐ Full-Time Student ☐ Part-Time Student ☐

CITY   **STATE**

ZIP CODE   **TELEPHONE** (Include Area Code) ( )

ZIP CODE   **TELEPHONE** (Include Area Code) ( )

9. OTHER INSURED'S NAME (Last Name, First Name, Middle Initial)

10. IS PATIENT'S CONDITION RELATED TO:

11. INSURED'S POLICY GROUP OR FECA NUMBER

a. OTHER INSURED'S POLICY OR GROUP NUMBER

a. EMPLOYMENT? (Current or Previous) ☐ YES ☐ NO

a. INSURED'S DATE OF BIRTH MM | DD | YY   **SEX** M ☐ F ☐

b. OTHER INSURED'S DATE OF BIRTH MM | DD | YY   **SEX** M ☐ F ☐

b. AUTO ACCIDENT? ☐ YES ☐ NO   **PLACE** (State)

b. EMPLOYER'S NAME OR SCHOOL NAME

c. EMPLOYER'S NAME OR SCHOOL NAME

c. OTHER ACCIDENT? ☐ YES ☐ NO

c. INSURANCE PLAN NAME OR PROGRAM NAME

d. INSURANCE PLAN NAME OR PROGRAM NAME

10d. RESERVED FOR LOCAL USE

d. IS THERE ANOTHER HEALTH BENEFIT PLAN? ☐ YES ☐ NO **If yes**, return to and complete item 9 a-d.

READ BACK OF FORM BEFORE COMPLETING & SIGNING THIS FORM.

12. PATIENT'S OR AUTHORIZED PERSON'S SIGNATURE I authorize the release of any medical or other information necessary to process this claim. I also request payment of government benefits either to myself or to the party who accepts assignment below.

SIGNED _____ DATE _____

13. INSURED'S OR AUTHORIZED PERSON'S SIGNATURE I authorize payment of medical benefits to the undersigned physician or supplier for services described below.

SIGNED _____

14. DATE OF CURRENT: MM | DD | YY   ◄ ILLNESS (First symptom) OR INJURY (Accident) OR PREGNANCY(LMP)

15. IF PATIENT HAS HAD SAME OR SIMILAR ILLNESS. GIVE FIRST DATE MM | DD | YY

16. DATES PATIENT UNABLE TO WORK IN CURRENT OCCUPATION MM | DD | YY   MM | DD | YY   FROM   TO

17. NAME OF REFERRING PROVIDER OR OTHER SOURCE

17a.

17b. NPI

18. HOSPITALIZATION DATES RELATED TO CURRENT SERVICES MM | DD | YY   MM | DD | YY   FROM   TO

19. RESERVED FOR LOCAL USE

20. OUTSIDE LAB? ☐ YES ☐ NO   **$ CHARGES**

21. DIAGNOSIS OR NATURE OF ILLNESS OR INJURY (Relate Items 1, 2, 3 or 4 to Item 24E by Line)

1. └___ . ___┘   3. └___ . ___┘

2. └___ . ___┘   4. └___ . ___┘

22. MEDICAID RESUBMISSION CODE   **ORIGINAL REF. NO.**

23. PRIOR AUTHORIZATION NUMBER

24. A. DATE(S) OF SERVICE From – To MM DD YY MM DD YY	B. PLACE OF SERVICE	C. EMG	D. PROCEDURES, SERVICES, OR SUPPLIES (Explain Unusual Circumstances) CPT/HCPCS MODIFIER	E. DIAGNOSIS POINTER	F. $ CHARGES	G. DAYS OR UNITS	H. EPSDT Family Plan	I. ID. QUAL.	J. RENDERING PROVIDER ID. #
1									NPI
2									NPI
3									NPI
4									NPI
5									NPI
6									NPI

25. FEDERAL TAX I.D. NUMBER SSN ☐ EIN ☐

26. PATIENT'S ACCOUNT NO.

27. ACCEPT ASSIGNMENT? (For govt. claims, see back) ☐ YES ☐ NO

28. TOTAL CHARGE $

29. AMOUNT PAID $

30. BALANCE DUE $

31. SIGNATURE OF PHYSICIAN OR SUPPLIER INCLUDING DEGREES OR CREDENTIALS (I certify that the statements on the reverse apply to this bill and are made a part thereof.)

SIGNED _____ DATE _____

32. SERVICE FACILITY LOCATION INFORMATION

a. NPI   b.

33. BILLING PROVIDER INFO & PH # ( )

a. NPI   b.

NUCC Instruction Manual available at: www.nucc.org   **PLEASE PRINT OR TYPE**   APPROVED OMB-0938-0999 FORM CMS-1500 (08-05)

Courtesy of Centers for Medicare & Medicaid Services.

CARRIER →

| | PICA | | | | | | | PICA | |

1. MEDICARE	MEDICAID	TRICARE CHAMPUS	CHAMPVA	GROUP HEALTH PLAN	FECA BLK LUNG	OTHER	1a. INSURED'S I.D. NUMBER	(For Program in Item 1)
(Medicare #)	(Medicaid #)	(Sponsor's SSN)	(Member ID#)	(SSN or ID)	(SSN)	(ID)		

2. PATIENT'S NAME (Last Name, First Name, Middle Initial)

3. PATIENT'S BIRTH DATE MM DD YY — SEX — M ☐ F ☐

4. INSURED'S NAME (Last Name, First Name, Middle Initial)

5. PATIENT'S ADDRESS (No., Street)

6. PATIENT RELATIONSHIP TO INSURED — Self ☐ Spouse ☐ Child ☐ Other ☐

7. INSURED'S ADDRESS (No., Street)

CITY | STATE

8. PATIENT STATUS — Single ☐ Married ☐ Other ☐

CITY | STATE

ZIP CODE | TELEPHONE (Include Area Code) ( )

Employed ☐ Full-Time Student ☐ Part-Time Student ☐

ZIP CODE | TELEPHONE (Include Area Code) ( )

9. OTHER INSURED'S NAME (Last Name, First Name, Middle Initial)

10. IS PATIENT'S CONDITION RELATED TO:

11. INSURED'S POLICY GROUP OR FECA NUMBER

a. OTHER INSURED'S POLICY OR GROUP NUMBER

a. EMPLOYMENT? (Current or Previous) — ☐ YES ☐ NO

a. INSURED'S DATE OF BIRTH MM DD YY — SEX — M ☐ F ☐

b. OTHER INSURED'S DATE OF BIRTH MM DD YY — SEX — M ☐ F ☐

b. AUTO ACCIDENT? PLACE (State) — ☐ YES ☐ NO

b. EMPLOYER'S NAME OR SCHOOL NAME

c. EMPLOYER'S NAME OR SCHOOL NAME

c. OTHER ACCIDENT? — ☐ YES ☐ NO

c. INSURANCE PLAN NAME OR PROGRAM NAME

d. INSURANCE PLAN NAME OR PROGRAM NAME

10d. RESERVED FOR LOCAL USE

d. IS THERE ANOTHER HEALTH BENEFIT PLAN? — ☐ YES ☐ NO *If yes*, return to and complete item 9 a-d.

READ BACK OF FORM BEFORE COMPLETING & SIGNING THIS FORM.

12. PATIENT'S OR AUTHORIZED PERSON'S SIGNATURE I authorize the release of any medical or other information necessary to process this claim. I also request payment of government benefits either to myself or to the party who accepts assignment below.

SIGNED _____ DATE _____

13. INSURED'S OR AUTHORIZED PERSON'S SIGNATURE I authorize payment of medical benefits to the undersigned physician or supplier for services described below.

SIGNED _____

← PATIENT AND INSURED INFORMATION

14. DATE OF CURRENT: MM DD YY ◄ ILLNESS (First symptom) OR INJURY (Accident) OR PREGNANCY(LMP)

15. IF PATIENT HAS HAD SAME OR SIMILAR ILLNESS. GIVE FIRST DATE MM DD YY

16. DATES PATIENT UNABLE TO WORK IN CURRENT OCCUPATION FROM MM DD YY TO MM DD YY

17. NAME OF REFERRING PROVIDER OR OTHER SOURCE

17a.

17b. NPI

18. HOSPITALIZATION DATES RELATED TO CURRENT SERVICES FROM MM DD YY TO MM DD YY

19. RESERVED FOR LOCAL USE

20. OUTSIDE LAB? ☐ YES ☐ NO | $ CHARGES

21. DIAGNOSIS OR NATURE OF ILLNESS OR INJURY (Relate Items 1, 2, 3 or 4 to Item 24E by Line)

1. |___.___
2. |___.___
3. |___.___
4. |___.___

22. MEDICAID RESUBMISSION CODE | ORIGINAL REF. NO.

23. PRIOR AUTHORIZATION NUMBER

24. A. DATE(S) OF SERVICE		B. PLACE OF SERVICE	C. EMG	D. PROCEDURES, SERVICES, OR SUPPLIES (Explain Unusual Circumstances) CPT/HCPCS MODIFIER	E. DIAGNOSIS POINTER	F. $ CHARGES	G. DAYS OR UNITS	H. EPSDT Family Plan	I. ID. QUAL.	J. RENDERING PROVIDER ID. #
From MM DD YY	To MM DD YY									
1									NPI	
2									NPI	
3									NPI	
4									NPI	
5									NPI	
6									NPI	

25. FEDERAL TAX I.D. NUMBER ☐ SSN ☐ EIN

26. PATIENT'S ACCOUNT NO.

27. ACCEPT ASSIGNMENT? (For govt. claims, see back) ☐ YES ☐ NO

28. TOTAL CHARGE $

29. AMOUNT PAID $

30. BALANCE DUE $

31. SIGNATURE OF PHYSICIAN OR SUPPLIER INCLUDING DEGREES OR CREDENTIALS (I certify that the statements on the reverse apply to this bill and are made a part thereof.)

SIGNED _____ DATE _____

32. SERVICE FACILITY LOCATION INFORMATION

a. NPI | b.

33. BILLING PROVIDER INFO & PH # ( )

a. NPI | b.

PHYSICIAN OR SUPPLIER INFORMATION →

1500

HEALTH INSURANCE CLAIM FORM

APPROVED BY NATIONAL UNIFORM CLAIM COMMITTEE 08/05

☐☐ PICA   PICA ☐☐

| 1. MEDICARE ☐ (Medicare #) MEDICAID ☐ (Medicaid #) TRICARE CHAMPUS ☐ (Sponsor's SSN) CHAMPVA ☐ (Member ID#) GROUP HEALTH PLAN ☐ (SSN or ID) FECA BLK LUNG ☐ (SSN) OTHER ☐ (ID) | 1a. INSURED'S I.D. NUMBER   (For Program in Item 1) |

2. PATIENT'S NAME (Last Name, First Name, Middle Initial)

3. PATIENT'S BIRTH DATE MM DD YY   SEX M ☐ F ☐

4. INSURED'S NAME (Last Name, First Name, Middle Initial)

5. PATIENT'S ADDRESS (No., Street)

6. PATIENT RELATIONSHIP TO INSURED Self ☐ Spouse ☐ Child ☐ Other ☐

7. INSURED'S ADDRESS (No., Street)

CITY   STATE

8. PATIENT STATUS Single ☐ Married ☐ Other ☐ Employed ☐ Full-Time Student ☐ Part-Time Student ☐

CITY   STATE

ZIP CODE   TELEPHONE (Include Area Code) ( )

ZIP CODE   TELEPHONE (Include Area Code) ( )

9. OTHER INSURED'S NAME (Last Name, First Name, Middle Initial)

10. IS PATIENT'S CONDITION RELATED TO:

11. INSURED'S POLICY GROUP OR FECA NUMBER

a. OTHER INSURED'S POLICY OR GROUP NUMBER

a. EMPLOYMENT? (Current or Previous) YES ☐ NO ☐

a. INSURED'S DATE OF BIRTH MM DD YY   SEX M ☐ F ☐

b. OTHER INSURED'S DATE OF BIRTH MM DD YY   SEX M ☐ F ☐

b. AUTO ACCIDENT?   PLACE (State) YES ☐ NO ☐

b. EMPLOYER'S NAME OR SCHOOL NAME

c. EMPLOYER'S NAME OR SCHOOL NAME

c. OTHER ACCIDENT? YES ☐ NO ☐

c. INSURANCE PLAN NAME OR PROGRAM NAME

d. INSURANCE PLAN NAME OR PROGRAM NAME

10d. RESERVED FOR LOCAL USE

d. IS THERE ANOTHER HEALTH BENEFIT PLAN? YES ☐ NO ☐ If yes, return to and complete item 9 a-d.

READ BACK OF FORM BEFORE COMPLETING & SIGNING THIS FORM.
12. PATIENT'S OR AUTHORIZED PERSON'S SIGNATURE I authorize the release of any medical or other information necessary to process this claim. I also request payment of government benefits either to myself or to the party who accepts assignment below.

SIGNED _____ DATE _____

13. INSURED'S OR AUTHORIZED PERSON'S SIGNATURE I authorize payment of medical benefits to the undersigned physician or supplier for services described below.

SIGNED _____

14. DATE OF CURRENT: MM DD YY ◄ ILLNESS (First symptom) OR INJURY (Accident) OR PREGNANCY(LMP)

15. IF PATIENT HAS HAD SAME OR SIMILAR ILLNESS. GIVE FIRST DATE MM DD YY

16. DATES PATIENT UNABLE TO WORK IN CURRENT OCCUPATION FROM MM DD YY TO MM DD YY

17. NAME OF REFERRING PROVIDER OR OTHER SOURCE

17a.
17b. NPI

18. HOSPITALIZATION DATES RELATED TO CURRENT SERVICES FROM MM DD YY TO MM DD YY

19. RESERVED FOR LOCAL USE

20. OUTSIDE LAB? YES ☐ NO ☐ $ CHARGES

21. DIAGNOSIS OR NATURE OF ILLNESS OR INJURY (Relate Items 1, 2, 3 or 4 to Item 24E by Line)

1. ____.____   3. ____.____

2. ____.____   4. ____.____

22. MEDICAID RESUBMISSION CODE ORIGINAL REF. NO.

23. PRIOR AUTHORIZATION NUMBER

24. A. DATE(S) OF SERVICE From MM DD YY To MM DD YY	B. PLACE OF SERVICE	C. EMG	D. PROCEDURES, SERVICES, OR SUPPLIES (Explain Unusual Circumstances) CPT/HCPCS	MODIFIER	E. DIAGNOSIS POINTER	F. $ CHARGES	G. DAYS OR UNITS	H. EPSDT Family Plan	I. ID. QUAL.	J. RENDERING PROVIDER ID. #
1									NPI	
2									NPI	
3									NPI	
4									NPI	
5									NPI	
6									NPI	

25. FEDERAL TAX I.D. NUMBER SSN ☐ EIN ☐

26. PATIENT'S ACCOUNT NO.

27. ACCEPT ASSIGNMENT? (For govt. claims, see back) YES ☐ NO ☐

28. TOTAL CHARGE $

29. AMOUNT PAID $

30. BALANCE DUE $

31. SIGNATURE OF PHYSICIAN OR SUPPLIER INCLUDING DEGREES OR CREDENTIALS (I certify that the statements on the reverse apply to this bill and are made a part thereof.)

SIGNED _____ DATE _____

32. SERVICE FACILITY LOCATION INFORMATION

a. NPI   b.

33. BILLING PROVIDER INFO & PH # ( )

a. NPI   b.

NUCC Instruction Manual available at: www.nucc.org   **PLEASE PRINT OR TYPE**   APPROVED OMB-0938-0999 FORM CMS-1500 (08-05)

Courtesy of Centers for Medicare & Medicaid Services.

1500

HEALTH INSURANCE CLAIM FORM

APPROVED BY NATIONAL UNIFORM CLAIM COMMITTEE 08/05

☐☐☐ PICA | | PICA ☐☐☐

1. MEDICARE ☐ (Medicare #)   MEDICAID ☐ (Medicaid #)   TRICARE CHAMPUS ☐ (Sponsor's SSN)   CHAMPVA ☐ (Member ID#)   GROUP HEALTH PLAN ☐ (SSN or ID)   FECA BLK LUNG ☐ (SSN)   OTHER ☐ (ID)

1a. INSURED'S I.D. NUMBER   (For Program in Item 1)

2. PATIENT'S NAME (Last Name, First Name, Middle Initial)

3. PATIENT'S BIRTH DATE   MM   DD   YY   SEX   M ☐   F ☐

4. INSURED'S NAME (Last Name, First Name, Middle Initial)

5. PATIENT'S ADDRESS (No., Street)

6. PATIENT RELATIONSHIP TO INSURED   Self ☐   Spouse ☐   Child ☐   Other ☐

7. INSURED'S ADDRESS (No., Street)

CITY   STATE

8. PATIENT STATUS   Single ☐   Married ☐   Other ☐   Employed ☐   Full-Time Student ☐   Part-Time Student ☐

CITY   STATE

ZIP CODE   TELEPHONE (Include Area Code) ( )

ZIP CODE   TELEPHONE (Include Area Code) ( )

9. OTHER INSURED'S NAME (Last Name, First Name, Middle Initial)

10. IS PATIENT'S CONDITION RELATED TO:

11. INSURED'S POLICY GROUP OR FECA NUMBER

a. OTHER INSURED'S POLICY OR GROUP NUMBER

a. EMPLOYMENT? (Current or Previous)   YES ☐   NO ☐

a. INSURED'S DATE OF BIRTH   MM   DD   YY   SEX   M ☐   F ☐

b. OTHER INSURED'S DATE OF BIRTH   MM   DD   YY   SEX   M ☐   F ☐

b. AUTO ACCIDENT?   PLACE (State)   YES ☐   NO ☐

b. EMPLOYER'S NAME OR SCHOOL NAME

c. EMPLOYER'S NAME OR SCHOOL NAME

c. OTHER ACCIDENT?   YES ☐   NO ☐

c. INSURANCE PLAN NAME OR PROGRAM NAME

d. INSURANCE PLAN NAME OR PROGRAM NAME

10d. RESERVED FOR LOCAL USE

d. IS THERE ANOTHER HEALTH BENEFIT PLAN?   YES ☐   NO ☐   *If yes*, return to and complete item 9 a-d.

READ BACK OF FORM BEFORE COMPLETING & SIGNING THIS FORM.

12. PATIENT'S OR AUTHORIZED PERSON'S SIGNATURE I authorize the release of any medical or other information necessary to process this claim. I also request payment of government benefits either to myself or to the party who accepts assignment below.

SIGNED _____ DATE _____

13. INSURED'S OR AUTHORIZED PERSON'S SIGNATURE I authorize payment of medical benefits to the undersigned physician or supplier for services described below.

SIGNED _____

14. DATE OF CURRENT: MM   DD   YY   ◄ ILLNESS (First symptom) OR INJURY (Accident) OR PREGNANCY(LMP)

15. IF PATIENT HAS HAD SAME OR SIMILAR ILLNESS. GIVE FIRST DATE   MM   DD   YY

16. DATES PATIENT UNABLE TO WORK IN CURRENT OCCUPATION   MM   DD   YY   FROM   MM   DD   YY   TO

17. NAME OF REFERRING PROVIDER OR OTHER SOURCE

17a.   **17b.** NPI

18. HOSPITALIZATION DATES RELATED TO CURRENT SERVICES   MM   DD   YY   FROM   MM   DD   YY   TO

19. RESERVED FOR LOCAL USE

20. OUTSIDE LAB?   YES ☐   NO ☐ $ CHARGES

21. DIAGNOSIS OR NATURE OF ILLNESS OR INJURY (Relate Items 1, 2, 3 or 4 to Item 24E by Line)

1. |___.___   3. |___.___

2. |___.___   4. |___.___

22. MEDICAID RESUBMISSION CODE   ORIGINAL REF. NO.

23. PRIOR AUTHORIZATION NUMBER

24. A. DATE(S) OF SERVICE From MM DD YY To MM DD YY	B. PLACE OF SERVICE	C. EMG	D. PROCEDURES, SERVICES, OR SUPPLIES (Explain Unusual Circumstances) CPT/HCPCS | MODIFIER	E. DIAGNOSIS POINTER	F. $ CHARGES	G. DAYS OR UNITS	H. EPSDT Family Plan	I. ID. QUAL.	J. RENDERING PROVIDER ID. #
1									NPI
2									NPI
3									NPI
4									NPI
5									NPI
6									NPI

25. FEDERAL TAX I.D. NUMBER   SSN ☐ EIN ☐

26. PATIENT'S ACCOUNT NO.

27. ACCEPT ASSIGNMENT? (For govt. claims, see back)   YES ☐   NO ☐

28. TOTAL CHARGE $

29. AMOUNT PAID $

30. BALANCE DUE $

31. SIGNATURE OF PHYSICIAN OR SUPPLIER INCLUDING DEGREES OR CREDENTIALS (I certify that the statements on the reverse apply to this bill and are made a part thereof.)

SIGNED _____ DATE _____

32. SERVICE FACILITY LOCATION INFORMATION

a.   b.

33. BILLING PROVIDER INFO & PH # ( )

a.   b.

NUCC Instruction Manual available at: www.nucc.org   **PLEASE PRINT OR TYPE**   APPROVED OMB-0938-0999 FORM CMS-1500 (08-05)

Courtesy of Centers for Medicare & Medicaid Services.

1500

HEALTH INSURANCE CLAIM FORM

APPROVED BY NATIONAL UNIFORM CLAIM COMMITTEE 08/05

◻◻◻ PICA

PICA ◻◻◻

1. MEDICARE ◻ (Medicare #)　MEDICAID ◻ (Medicaid #)　TRICARE CHAMPUS ◻ (Sponsor's SSN)　CHAMPVA ◻ (Member ID#)　GROUP HEALTH PLAN ◻ (SSN or ID)　FECA BLK LUNG ◻ (SSN)　OTHER ◻ (ID)

1a. INSURED'S I.D. NUMBER　(For Program in Item 1)

2. PATIENT'S NAME (Last Name, First Name, Middle Initial)

3. PATIENT'S BIRTH DATE　MM ⎜ DD ⎜ YY　SEX　M ◻　F ◻

4. INSURED'S NAME (Last Name, First Name, Middle Initial)

5. PATIENT'S ADDRESS (No., Street)

6. PATIENT RELATIONSHIP TO INSURED
Self ◻　Spouse ◻　Child ◻　Other ◻

7. INSURED'S ADDRESS (No., Street)

CITY　STATE

8. PATIENT STATUS
Single ◻　Married ◻　Other ◻

CITY　STATE

ZIP CODE　TELEPHONE (Include Area Code)　(　)

Employed ◻　Full-Time Student ◻　Part-Time Student ◻

ZIP CODE　TELEPHONE (Include Area Code)　(　)

9. OTHER INSURED'S NAME (Last Name, First Name, Middle Initial)

10. IS PATIENT'S CONDITION RELATED TO:

11. INSURED'S POLICY GROUP OR FECA NUMBER

a. OTHER INSURED'S POLICY OR GROUP NUMBER

a. EMPLOYMENT? (Current or Previous)
◻ YES　◻ NO

a. INSURED'S DATE OF BIRTH　MM ⎜ DD ⎜ YY　SEX　M ◻　F ◻

b. OTHER INSURED'S DATE OF BIRTH　MM ⎜ DD ⎜ YY　SEX　M ◻　F ◻

b. AUTO ACCIDENT?　PLACE (State)
◻ YES　◻ NO

b. EMPLOYER'S NAME OR SCHOOL NAME

c. EMPLOYER'S NAME OR SCHOOL NAME

c. OTHER ACCIDENT?
◻ YES　◻ NO

c. INSURANCE PLAN NAME OR PROGRAM NAME

d. INSURANCE PLAN NAME OR PROGRAM NAME

10d. RESERVED FOR LOCAL USE

d. IS THERE ANOTHER HEALTH BENEFIT PLAN?
◻ YES　◻ NO　If yes, return to and complete item 9 a-d.

READ BACK OF FORM BEFORE COMPLETING & SIGNING THIS FORM.

12. PATIENT'S OR AUTHORIZED PERSON'S SIGNATURE I authorize the release of any medical or other information necessary to process this claim. I also request payment of government benefits either to myself or to the party who accepts assignment below.

SIGNED _____　DATE _____

13. INSURED'S OR AUTHORIZED PERSON'S SIGNATURE I authorize payment of medical benefits to the undersigned physician or supplier for services described below.

SIGNED _____

14. DATE OF CURRENT:　MM ⎜ DD ⎜ YY　◀ ILLNESS (First symptom) OR INJURY (Accident) OR PREGNANCY(LMP)

15. IF PATIENT HAS HAD SAME OR SIMILAR ILLNESS. GIVE FIRST DATE　MM ⎜ DD ⎜ YY

16. DATES PATIENT UNABLE TO WORK IN CURRENT OCCUPATION
FROM　MM ⎜ DD ⎜ YY　TO　MM ⎜ DD ⎜ YY

17. NAME OF REFERRING PROVIDER OR OTHER SOURCE

17a.
17b. NPI

18. HOSPITALIZATION DATES RELATED TO CURRENT SERVICES
FROM　MM ⎜ DD ⎜ YY　TO　MM ⎜ DD ⎜ YY

19. RESERVED FOR LOCAL USE

20. OUTSIDE LAB?　$ CHARGES
◻ YES　◻ NO

21. DIAGNOSIS OR NATURE OF ILLNESS OR INJURY (Relate Items 1, 2, 3 or 4 to Item 24E by Line)

1. ⌞__⌟ . __　3. ⌞__⌟ . __

2. ⌞__⌟ . __　4. ⌞__⌟ . __

22. MEDICAID RESUBMISSION CODE　ORIGINAL REF. NO.

23. PRIOR AUTHORIZATION NUMBER

24. A. DATE(S) OF SERVICE		B. PLACE OF SERVICE	C. EMG	D. PROCEDURES, SERVICES, OR SUPPLIES (Explain Unusual Circumstances)		E. DIAGNOSIS POINTER	F. $ CHARGES	G. DAYS OR UNITS	H. EPSDT Family Plan	I. ID. QUAL.	J. RENDERING PROVIDER ID. #
From MM DD YY	To MM DD YY			CPT/HCPCS	MODIFIER						
1										NPI	
2										NPI	
3										NPI	
4										NPI	
5										NPI	
6										NPI	

25. FEDERAL TAX I.D. NUMBER　SSN ◻ EIN ◻

26. PATIENT'S ACCOUNT NO.

27. ACCEPT ASSIGNMENT? (For govt. claims, see back)　◻ YES　◻ NO

28. TOTAL CHARGE　$

29. AMOUNT PAID　$

30. BALANCE DUE　$

31. SIGNATURE OF PHYSICIAN OR SUPPLIER INCLUDING DEGREES OR CREDENTIALS (I certify that the statements on the reverse apply to this bill and are made a part thereof.)

SIGNED _____　DATE _____

32. SERVICE FACILITY LOCATION INFORMATION

a. ____　b. ____

33. BILLING PROVIDER INFO & PH # (　)

a. ____　b. ____

NUCC Instruction Manual available at: www.nucc.org　**PLEASE PRINT OR TYPE**　APPROVED OMB-0938-0999 FORM CMS-1500 (08-05)

Courtesy of Centers for Medicare & Medicaid Services.

1500

HEALTH INSURANCE CLAIM FORM

APPROVED BY NATIONAL UNIFORM CLAIM COMMITTEE 08/05

☐☐☐ PICA   PICA ☐☐☐

1. MEDICARE	MEDICAID	TRICARE CHAMPUS	CHAMPVA	GROUP HEALTH PLAN	FECA BLK LUNG	OTHER	1a. INSURED'S I.D. NUMBER	(For Program in Item 1)
☐ (Medicare #)	☐ (Medicaid #)	☐ (Sponsor's SSN)	☐ (Member ID#)	☐ (SSN or ID)	☐ (SSN)	☐ (ID)		

2. PATIENT'S NAME (Last Name, First Name, Middle Initial)

3. PATIENT'S BIRTH DATE MM DD YY   SEX   M ☐ F ☐

4. INSURED'S NAME (Last Name, First Name, Middle Initial)

5. PATIENT'S ADDRESS (No., Street)

6. PATIENT RELATIONSHIP TO INSURED
Self ☐ Spouse ☐ Child ☐ Other ☐

7. INSURED'S ADDRESS (No., Street)

CITY   STATE

8. PATIENT STATUS
Single ☐ Married ☐ Other ☐
Employed ☐ Full-Time Student ☐ Part-Time Student ☐

CITY   STATE

ZIP CODE   TELEPHONE (Include Area Code) ( )

ZIP CODE   TELEPHONE (Include Area Code) ( )

9. OTHER INSURED'S NAME (Last Name, First Name, Middle Initial)

10. IS PATIENT'S CONDITION RELATED TO:

11. INSURED'S POLICY GROUP OR FECA NUMBER

a. OTHER INSURED'S POLICY OR GROUP NUMBER

a. EMPLOYMENT? (Current or Previous) ☐ YES ☐ NO

a. INSURED'S DATE OF BIRTH MM DD YY   SEX   M ☐ F ☐

b. OTHER INSURED'S DATE OF BIRTH MM DD YY   SEX M ☐ F ☐

b. AUTO ACCIDENT?   PLACE (State) ☐ YES ☐ NO

b. EMPLOYER'S NAME OR SCHOOL NAME

c. EMPLOYER'S NAME OR SCHOOL NAME

c. OTHER ACCIDENT? ☐ YES ☐ NO

c. INSURANCE PLAN NAME OR PROGRAM NAME

d. INSURANCE PLAN NAME OR PROGRAM NAME

10d. RESERVED FOR LOCAL USE

d. IS THERE ANOTHER HEALTH BENEFIT PLAN?
☐ YES ☐ NO   *If yes*, return to and complete item 9 a-d.

READ BACK OF FORM BEFORE COMPLETING & SIGNING THIS FORM.

12. PATIENT'S OR AUTHORIZED PERSON'S SIGNATURE I authorize the release of any medical or other information necessary to process this claim. I also request payment of government benefits either to myself or to the party who accepts assignment below.

SIGNED _____ DATE _____

13. INSURED'S OR AUTHORIZED PERSON'S SIGNATURE I authorize payment of medical benefits to the undersigned physician or supplier for services described below.

SIGNED _____

14. DATE OF CURRENT: MM DD YY   ◄ ILLNESS (First symptom) OR INJURY (Accident) OR PREGNANCY(LMP)

15. IF PATIENT HAS HAD SAME OR SIMILAR ILLNESS. GIVE FIRST DATE MM DD YY

16. DATES PATIENT UNABLE TO WORK IN CURRENT OCCUPATION MM DD YY   FROM   TO MM DD YY

17. NAME OF REFERRING PROVIDER OR OTHER SOURCE

17a.
17b. NPI

18. HOSPITALIZATION DATES RELATED TO CURRENT SERVICES MM DD YY FROM   TO MM DD YY

19. RESERVED FOR LOCAL USE

20. OUTSIDE LAB? ☐ YES ☐ NO $ CHARGES

21. DIAGNOSIS OR NATURE OF ILLNESS OR INJURY (Relate Items 1, 2, 3 or 4 to Item 24E by Line)

1. �'__ . __
2. �'__ . __
3. �'__ . __
4. �'__ . __

22. MEDICAID RESUBMISSION CODE   ORIGINAL REF. NO.

23. PRIOR AUTHORIZATION NUMBER

24. A. DATE(S) OF SERVICE From MM DD YY To MM DD YY	B. PLACE OF SERVICE	C. EMG	D. PROCEDURES, SERVICES, OR SUPPLIES (Explain Unusual Circumstances) CPT/HCPCS | MODIFIER	E. DIAGNOSIS POINTER	F. $ CHARGES	G. DAYS OR UNITS	H. EPSDT Family Plan	I. ID. QUAL.	J. RENDERING PROVIDER ID. #
1									NPI
2									NPI
3									NPI
4									NPI
5									NPI
6									NPI

25. FEDERAL TAX I.D. NUMBER SSN EIN ☐☐

26. PATIENT'S ACCOUNT NO.

27. ACCEPT ASSIGNMENT? (For govt. claims, see back) ☐ YES ☐ NO

28. TOTAL CHARGE $

29. AMOUNT PAID $

30. BALANCE DUE $

31. SIGNATURE OF PHYSICIAN OR SUPPLIER INCLUDING DEGREES OR CREDENTIALS (I certify that the statements on the reverse apply to this bill and are made a part thereof.)

SIGNED _____ DATE _____

32. SERVICE FACILITY LOCATION INFORMATION

a.   b.

33. BILLING PROVIDER INFO & PH # ( )

a.   b.

NUCC Instruction Manual available at: www.nucc.org   **PLEASE PRINT OR TYPE**   APPROVED OMB-0938-0999 FORM CMS-1500 (08-05)

Courtesy of Centers for Medicare & Medicaid Services.

1500

HEALTH INSURANCE CLAIM FORM

APPROVED BY NATIONAL UNIFORM CLAIM COMMITTEE 08/05

PICA | | | | | | | | | | | PICA | |

1. MEDICARE ☐ *(Medicare #)* MEDICAID ☐ *(Medicaid #)* TRICARE CHAMPUS ☐ *(Sponsor's SSN)* CHAMPVA ☐ *(Member ID#)* GROUP HEALTH PLAN ☐ *(SSN or ID)* FECA BLK LUNG ☐ *(SSN)* OTHER ☐ *(ID)*

1a. INSURED'S I.D. NUMBER *(For Program in Item 1)*

2. PATIENT'S NAME (Last Name, First Name, Middle Initial)

3. PATIENT'S BIRTH DATE MM DD YY SEX M ☐ F ☐

4. INSURED'S NAME (Last Name, First Name, Middle Initial)

5. PATIENT'S ADDRESS (No., Street)

6. PATIENT RELATIONSHIP TO INSURED Self ☐ Spouse ☐ Child ☐ Other ☐

7. INSURED'S ADDRESS (No., Street)

CITY | STATE

8. PATIENT STATUS Single ☐ Married ☐ Other ☐ Employed ☐ Full-Time Student ☐ Part-Time Student ☐

CITY | STATE

ZIP CODE | TELEPHONE (Include Area Code) ( )

ZIP CODE | TELEPHONE (Include Area Code) ( )

9. OTHER INSURED'S NAME (Last Name, First Name, Middle Initial)

10. IS PATIENT'S CONDITION RELATED TO:

11. INSURED'S POLICY GROUP OR FECA NUMBER

a. OTHER INSURED'S POLICY OR GROUP NUMBER

a. EMPLOYMENT? (Current or Previous) ☐ YES ☐ NO

a. INSURED'S DATE OF BIRTH MM DD YY SEX M ☐ F ☐

b. OTHER INSURED'S DATE OF BIRTH MM DD YY SEX M ☐ F ☐

b. AUTO ACCIDENT? PLACE (State) ☐ YES ☐ NO

b. EMPLOYER'S NAME OR SCHOOL NAME

c. EMPLOYER'S NAME OR SCHOOL NAME

c. OTHER ACCIDENT? ☐ YES ☐ NO

c. INSURANCE PLAN NAME OR PROGRAM NAME

d. INSURANCE PLAN NAME OR PROGRAM NAME

10d. RESERVED FOR LOCAL USE

d. IS THERE ANOTHER HEALTH BENEFIT PLAN? ☐ YES ☐ NO *If yes*, return to and complete item 9 a-d.

READ BACK OF FORM BEFORE COMPLETING & SIGNING THIS FORM.
12. PATIENT'S OR AUTHORIZED PERSON'S SIGNATURE I authorize the release of any medical or other information necessary to process this claim. I also request payment of government benefits either to myself or to the party who accepts assignment below.

SIGNED _____ DATE _____

13. INSURED'S OR AUTHORIZED PERSON'S SIGNATURE I authorize payment of medical benefits to the undersigned physician or supplier for services described below.

SIGNED _____

14. DATE OF CURRENT: ILLNESS (First symptom) OR INJURY (Accident) OR PREGNANCY(LMP) MM DD YY

15. IF PATIENT HAS HAD SAME OR SIMILAR ILLNESS. GIVE FIRST DATE MM DD YY

16. DATES PATIENT UNABLE TO WORK IN CURRENT OCCUPATION FROM MM DD YY TO MM DD YY

17. NAME OF REFERRING PROVIDER OR OTHER SOURCE | **17a.** | **17b.** NPI

18. HOSPITALIZATION DATES RELATED TO CURRENT SERVICES FROM MM DD YY TO MM DD YY

19. RESERVED FOR LOCAL USE

20. OUTSIDE LAB? ☐ YES ☐ NO | $ CHARGES

21. DIAGNOSIS OR NATURE OF ILLNESS OR INJURY (Relate Items 1, 2, 3 or 4 to Item 24E by Line)

1. |___.___ 3. |___.___
2. |___.___ 4. |___.___

22. MEDICAID RESUBMISSION CODE | ORIGINAL REF. NO.

23. PRIOR AUTHORIZATION NUMBER

24. A. DATE(S) OF SERVICE		B. PLACE OF SERVICE	C. EMG	D. PROCEDURES, SERVICES, OR SUPPLIES (Explain Unusual Circumstances)		E. DIAGNOSIS POINTER	F. $ CHARGES	G. DAYS OR UNITS	H. EPSDT Family Plan	I. ID. QUAL.	J. RENDERING PROVIDER ID. #
From MM DD YY	To MM DD YY			CPT/HCPCS	MODIFIER						
1											NPI
2											NPI
3											NPI
4											NPI
5											NPI
6											NPI

25. FEDERAL TAX I.D. NUMBER SSN ☐ EIN ☐

26. PATIENT'S ACCOUNT NO.

27. ACCEPT ASSIGNMENT? (For govt. claims, see back) ☐ YES ☐ NO

28. TOTAL CHARGE $

29. AMOUNT PAID $

30. BALANCE DUE $

31. SIGNATURE OF PHYSICIAN OR SUPPLIER INCLUDING DEGREES OR CREDENTIALS (I certify that the statements on the reverse apply to this bill and are made a part thereof.)

SIGNED _____ DATE _____

32. SERVICE FACILITY LOCATION INFORMATION

a. b.

33. BILLING PROVIDER INFO & PH # ( )

a. b.

NUCC Instruction Manual available at: www.nucc.org

PLEASE PRINT OR TYPE

APPROVED OMB-0938-0999 FORM CMS-1500 (08-05)

Courtesy of Centers for Medicare & Medicaid Services.

1500

HEALTH INSURANCE CLAIM FORM

APPROVED BY NATIONAL UNIFORM CLAIM COMMITTEE 08/05

☐☐☐ PICA

PICA ☐☐☐

| 1. MEDICARE ☐ (Medicare #) | MEDICAID ☐ (Medicaid #) | TRICARE CHAMPUS ☐ (Sponsor's SSN) | CHAMPVA ☐ (Member ID#) | GROUP HEALTH PLAN ☐ (SSN or ID) | FECA BLK LUNG ☐ (SSN) | OTHER ☐ (ID) | 1a. INSURED'S I.D. NUMBER (For Program in Item 1) |

2. PATIENT'S NAME (Last Name, First Name, Middle Initial)

3. PATIENT'S BIRTH DATE MM | DD | YY   SEX   M ☐   F ☐

4. INSURED'S NAME (Last Name, First Name, Middle Initial)

5. PATIENT'S ADDRESS (No., Street)

6. PATIENT RELATIONSHIP TO INSURED
Self ☐   Spouse ☐   Child ☐   Other ☐

7. INSURED'S ADDRESS (No., Street)

CITY   STATE

8. PATIENT STATUS
Single ☐   Married ☐   Other ☐

CITY   STATE

ZIP CODE   TELEPHONE (Include Area Code) ( )

Employed ☐   Full-Time Student ☐   Part-Time Student ☐

ZIP CODE   TELEPHONE (Include Area Code) ( )

9. OTHER INSURED'S NAME (Last Name, First Name, Middle Initial)

10. IS PATIENT'S CONDITION RELATED TO:

11. INSURED'S POLICY GROUP OR FECA NUMBER

a. OTHER INSURED'S POLICY OR GROUP NUMBER

a. EMPLOYMENT? (Current or Previous) ☐ YES ☐ NO

a. INSURED'S DATE OF BIRTH MM | DD | YY   SEX   M ☐   F ☐

b. OTHER INSURED'S DATE OF BIRTH MM | DD | YY   SEX   M ☐   F ☐

b. AUTO ACCIDENT?   PLACE (State) ☐ YES ☐ NO

b. EMPLOYER'S NAME OR SCHOOL NAME

c. EMPLOYER'S NAME OR SCHOOL NAME

c. OTHER ACCIDENT? ☐ YES ☐ NO

c. INSURANCE PLAN NAME OR PROGRAM NAME

d. INSURANCE PLAN NAME OR PROGRAM NAME

10d. RESERVED FOR LOCAL USE

d. IS THERE ANOTHER HEALTH BENEFIT PLAN?
☐ YES ☐ NO   If yes, return to and complete item 9 a-d.

READ BACK OF FORM BEFORE COMPLETING & SIGNING THIS FORM.
12. PATIENT'S OR AUTHORIZED PERSON'S SIGNATURE I authorize the release of any medical or other information necessary to process this claim. I also request payment of government benefits either to myself or to the party who accepts assignment below.

SIGNED _____ DATE _____

13. INSURED'S OR AUTHORIZED PERSON'S SIGNATURE I authorize payment of medical benefits to the undersigned physician or supplier for services described below.

SIGNED _____

14. DATE OF CURRENT: MM | DD | YY ◄ ILLNESS (First symptom) OR INJURY (Accident) OR PREGNANCY(LMP)

15. IF PATIENT HAS HAD SAME OR SIMILAR ILLNESS. GIVE FIRST DATE MM | DD | YY

16. DATES PATIENT UNABLE TO WORK IN CURRENT OCCUPATION MM | DD | YY   MM | DD | YY
FROM   TO

17. NAME OF REFERRING PROVIDER OR OTHER SOURCE

17a.
17b. NPI

18. HOSPITALIZATION DATES RELATED TO CURRENT SERVICES MM | DD | YY   MM | DD | YY
FROM   TO

19. RESERVED FOR LOCAL USE

20. OUTSIDE LAB? $ CHARGES
☐ YES ☐ NO

21. DIAGNOSIS OR NATURE OF ILLNESS OR INJURY (Relate Items 1, 2, 3 or 4 to Item 24E by Line)

1. |___.___   3. |___.___

2. |___.___   4. |___.___

22. MEDICAID RESUBMISSION CODE   ORIGINAL REF. NO.

23. PRIOR AUTHORIZATION NUMBER

24. A. DATE(S) OF SERVICE From MM DD YY To MM DD YY	B. PLACE OF SERVICE	C. EMG	D. PROCEDURES, SERVICES, OR SUPPLIES (Explain Unusual Circumstances) CPT/HCPCS	MODIFIER	E. DIAGNOSIS POINTER	F. $ CHARGES	G. DAYS OR UNITS	H. EPSDT Family Plan	I. ID. QUAL.	J. RENDERING PROVIDER ID. #
1										NPI
2										NPI
3										NPI
4										NPI
5										NPI
6										NPI

25. FEDERAL TAX I.D. NUMBER   SSN ☐ EIN ☐

26. PATIENT'S ACCOUNT NO.

27. ACCEPT ASSIGNMENT? (For govt. claims, see back) ☐ YES ☐ NO

28. TOTAL CHARGE $

29. AMOUNT PAID $

30. BALANCE DUE $

31. SIGNATURE OF PHYSICIAN OR SUPPLIER INCLUDING DEGREES OR CREDENTIALS (I certify that the statements on the reverse apply to this bill and are made a part thereof.)

SIGNED _____ DATE _____

32. SERVICE FACILITY LOCATION INFORMATION

a.   b.

33. BILLING PROVIDER INFO & PH # ( )

a.   b.

NUCC Instruction Manual available at: www.nucc.org   **PLEASE PRINT OR TYPE**   APPROVED OMB-0938-0999 FORM CMS-1500 (08-05)

Courtesy of Centers for Medicare & Medicaid Services.

1500

HEALTH INSURANCE CLAIM FORM

APPROVED BY NATIONAL UNIFORM CLAIM COMMITTEE 08/05

PICA □□□ | PICA □□□

1. MEDICARE (Medicare #) □ **MEDICAID** (Medicaid #) □ **TRICARE CHAMPUS** (Sponsor's SSN) □ **CHAMPVA** (Member ID#) □ **GROUP HEALTH PLAN** (SSN or ID) □ **FECA BLK LUNG** (SSN) □ **OTHER** (ID) □

1a. INSURED'S I.D. NUMBER (For Program in Item 1)

2. PATIENT'S NAME (Last Name, First Name, Middle Initial)

3. PATIENT'S BIRTH DATE MM DD YY **SEX** M □ F □

4. INSURED'S NAME (Last Name, First Name, Middle Initial)

5. PATIENT'S ADDRESS (No., Street)

6. PATIENT RELATIONSHIP TO INSURED Self □ Spouse □ Child □ Other □

7. INSURED'S ADDRESS (No., Street)

CITY | STATE

8. PATIENT STATUS Single □ Married □ Other □

CITY | STATE

ZIP CODE | TELEPHONE (Include Area Code) ( )

Employed □ Full-Time Student □ Part-Time Student □

ZIP CODE | TELEPHONE (Include Area Code) ( )

9. OTHER INSURED'S NAME (Last Name, First Name, Middle Initial)

10. IS PATIENT'S CONDITION RELATED TO:

11. INSURED'S POLICY GROUP OR FECA NUMBER

a. OTHER INSURED'S POLICY OR GROUP NUMBER

a. EMPLOYMENT? (Current or Previous) YES □ NO □

a. INSURED'S DATE OF BIRTH MM DD YY **SEX** M □ F □

b. OTHER INSURED'S DATE OF BIRTH MM DD YY **SEX** M □ F □

b. AUTO ACCIDENT? YES □ NO □ **PLACE (State)**

b. EMPLOYER'S NAME OR SCHOOL NAME

c. EMPLOYER'S NAME OR SCHOOL NAME

c. OTHER ACCIDENT? YES □ NO □

c. INSURANCE PLAN NAME OR PROGRAM NAME

d. INSURANCE PLAN NAME OR PROGRAM NAME

10d. RESERVED FOR LOCAL USE

d. IS THERE ANOTHER HEALTH BENEFIT PLAN? YES □ NO □ *If yes*, return to and complete item 9 a-d.

READ BACK OF FORM BEFORE COMPLETING & SIGNING THIS FORM.
12. PATIENT'S OR AUTHORIZED PERSON'S SIGNATURE I authorize the release of any medical or other information necessary to process this claim. I also request payment of government benefits either to myself or to the party who accepts assignment below.

SIGNED _____ DATE _____

13. INSURED'S OR AUTHORIZED PERSON'S SIGNATURE I authorize payment of medical benefits to the undersigned physician or supplier for services described below.

SIGNED _____

14. DATE OF CURRENT: MM DD YY ◄ ILLNESS (First symptom) OR INJURY (Accident) OR PREGNANCY(LMP)

15. IF PATIENT HAS HAD SAME OR SIMILAR ILLNESS. GIVE FIRST DATE MM DD YY

16. DATES PATIENT UNABLE TO WORK IN CURRENT OCCUPATION FROM MM DD YY TO MM DD YY

17. NAME OF REFERRING PROVIDER OR OTHER SOURCE

17a. | 17b. NPI

18. HOSPITALIZATION DATES RELATED TO CURRENT SERVICES FROM MM DD YY TO MM DD YY

19. RESERVED FOR LOCAL USE

20. OUTSIDE LAB? YES □ NO □ **$ CHARGES**

21. DIAGNOSIS OR NATURE OF ILLNESS OR INJURY (Relate Items 1, 2, 3 or 4 to Item 24E by Line)

1. |___.___
2. |___.___
3. |___.___
4. |___.___

22. MEDICAID RESUBMISSION CODE | ORIGINAL REF. NO.

23. PRIOR AUTHORIZATION NUMBER

24. A. DATE(S) OF SERVICE		B. PLACE OF SERVICE	C. EMG	D. PROCEDURES, SERVICES, OR SUPPLIES (Explain Unusual Circumstances)		E. DIAGNOSIS POINTER	F. $ CHARGES	G. DAYS OR UNITS	H. EPSDT Family Plan	I. ID. QUAL.	J. RENDERING PROVIDER ID. #
From MM DD YY	To MM DD YY			CPT/HCPCS	MODIFIER						
1										NPI	
2										NPI	
3										NPI	
4										NPI	
5										NPI	
6										NPI	

25. FEDERAL TAX I.D. NUMBER SSN □ EIN □

26. PATIENT'S ACCOUNT NO.

27. ACCEPT ASSIGNMENT? (For govt. claims, see back) YES □ NO □

28. TOTAL CHARGE $

29. AMOUNT PAID $

30. BALANCE DUE $

31. SIGNATURE OF PHYSICIAN OR SUPPLIER INCLUDING DEGREES OR CREDENTIALS (I certify that the statements on the reverse apply to this bill and are made a part thereof.)

SIGNED _____ DATE _____

32. SERVICE FACILITY LOCATION INFORMATION

a. NPI | b.

33. BILLING PROVIDER INFO & PH # ( )

a. NPI | b.

NUCC Instruction Manual available at: www.nucc.org | **PLEASE PRINT OR TYPE** | APPROVED OMB-0938-0999 FORM CMS-1500 (08-05)

Courtesy of Centers for Medicare & Medicaid Services.

1500

HEALTH INSURANCE CLAIM FORM

APPROVED BY NATIONAL UNIFORM CLAIM COMMITTEE 08/05

☐☐☐ PICA

PICA ☐☐☐

1. MEDICARE ☐ (Medicare #)	MEDICAID ☐ (Medicaid #)	TRICARE CHAMPUS ☐ (Sponsor's SSN)	CHAMPVA ☐ (Member ID#)	GROUP HEALTH PLAN ☐ (SSN or ID)	FECA BLK LUNG ☐ (SSN)	OTHER ☐ (ID)	1a. INSURED'S I.D. NUMBER	(For Program in Item 1)

2. PATIENT'S NAME (Last Name, First Name, Middle Initial)

3. PATIENT'S BIRTH DATE MM ┊ DD ┊ YY **SEX** M ☐ F ☐

4. INSURED'S NAME (Last Name, First Name, Middle Initial)

5. PATIENT'S ADDRESS (No., Street)

6. PATIENT RELATIONSHIP TO INSURED Self ☐ Spouse ☐ Child ☐ Other ☐

7. INSURED'S ADDRESS (No., Street)

CITY ┊ STATE

8. PATIENT STATUS Single ☐ Married ☐ Other ☐

CITY ┊ STATE

ZIP CODE ┊ TELEPHONE (Include Area Code) ( )

Employed ☐ Full-Time Student ☐ Part-Time Student ☐

ZIP CODE ┊ TELEPHONE (Include Area Code) ( )

9. OTHER INSURED'S NAME (Last Name, First Name, Middle Initial)

10. IS PATIENT'S CONDITION RELATED TO:

11. INSURED'S POLICY GROUP OR FECA NUMBER

a. OTHER INSURED'S POLICY OR GROUP NUMBER

a. EMPLOYMENT? (Current or Previous) YES ☐ NO ☐

a. INSURED'S DATE OF BIRTH MM ┊ DD ┊ YY **SEX** M ☐ F ☐

b. OTHER INSURED'S DATE OF BIRTH MM ┊ DD ┊ YY **SEX** M ☐ F ☐

b. AUTO ACCIDENT? YES ☐ NO ☐ PLACE (State) ┊

b. EMPLOYER'S NAME OR SCHOOL NAME

c. EMPLOYER'S NAME OR SCHOOL NAME

c. OTHER ACCIDENT? YES ☐ NO ☐

c. INSURANCE PLAN NAME OR PROGRAM NAME

d. INSURANCE PLAN NAME OR PROGRAM NAME

10d. RESERVED FOR LOCAL USE

d. IS THERE ANOTHER HEALTH BENEFIT PLAN? YES ☐ NO ☐ *If yes*, return to and complete item 9 a-d.

READ BACK OF FORM BEFORE COMPLETING & SIGNING THIS FORM.
12. PATIENT'S OR AUTHORIZED PERSON'S SIGNATURE I authorize the release of any medical or other information necessary to process this claim. I also request payment of government benefits either to myself or to the party who accepts assignment below.

SIGNED _____ DATE _____

13. INSURED'S OR AUTHORIZED PERSON'S SIGNATURE I authorize payment of medical benefits to the undersigned physician or supplier for services described below.

SIGNED _____

14. DATE OF CURRENT: MM ┊ DD ┊ YY ◄ ILLNESS (First symptom) OR INJURY (Accident) OR PREGNANCY(LMP)

15. IF PATIENT HAS HAD SAME OR SIMILAR ILLNESS. GIVE FIRST DATE MM ┊ DD ┊ YY

16. DATES PATIENT UNABLE TO WORK IN CURRENT OCCUPATION MM ┊ DD ┊ YY FROM ┊ TO MM ┊ DD ┊ YY

17. NAME OF REFERRING PROVIDER OR OTHER SOURCE

17a.
17b. NPI

18. HOSPITALIZATION DATES RELATED TO CURRENT SERVICES MM ┊ DD ┊ YY FROM ┊ TO MM ┊ DD ┊ YY

19. RESERVED FOR LOCAL USE

20. OUTSIDE LAB? YES ☐ NO ☐ $ CHARGES

21. DIAGNOSIS OR NATURE OF ILLNESS OR INJURY (Relate Items 1, 2, 3 or 4 to Item 24E by Line)

1. └─┘ . └─┘
2. └─┘ . └─┘
3. └─┘ . └─┘
4. └─┘ . └─┘

22. MEDICAID RESUBMISSION CODE ┊ ORIGINAL REF. NO.

23. PRIOR AUTHORIZATION NUMBER

24. A. DATE(S) OF SERVICE From MM DD YY — To MM DD YY	B. PLACE OF SERVICE	C. EMG	D. PROCEDURES, SERVICES, OR SUPPLIES (Explain Unusual Circumstances) CPT/HCPCS ┊ MODIFIER	E. DIAGNOSIS POINTER	F. $ CHARGES	G. DAYS OR UNITS	H. EPSDT Family Plan	I. ID. QUAL.	J. RENDERING PROVIDER ID. #
1									NPI
2									NPI
3									NPI
4									NPI
5									NPI
6									NPI

25. FEDERAL TAX I.D. NUMBER SSN ☐ EIN ☐

26. PATIENT'S ACCOUNT NO.

27. ACCEPT ASSIGNMENT? (For govt. claims, see back) YES ☐ NO ☐

28. TOTAL CHARGE $

29. AMOUNT PAID $

30. BALANCE DUE $

31. SIGNATURE OF PHYSICIAN OR SUPPLIER INCLUDING DEGREES OR CREDENTIALS (I certify that the statements on the reverse apply to this bill and are made a part thereof.)

SIGNED _____ DATE _____

32. SERVICE FACILITY LOCATION INFORMATION

a. ┊ b.

33. BILLING PROVIDER INFO & PH # ( )

a. ┊ b.

NUCC Instruction Manual available at: www.nucc.org   **PLEASE PRINT OR TYPE**   APPROVED OMB-0938-0999 FORM CMS-1500 (08-05)